Apocalypse Now

Scene-by-Scene

Apocalypse Now

Scene-by-Scene

John David Ebert

ISBN: 978-0-9854802-8-8

Post Egoism Media | Eugene, Oregon

Acknowledgements

Special thanks go to JD Casten and Michael Aaron Kamins for their help with encouraging this manuscript. Thanks are also due to my brother Thomas Ebert for designing the cover. And also thanks, yet again, to John Lobell, whose patronage has allowed my website cinemadiscourse.com to exist all these years.

Cover artwork:
"Morning in the Tropics" by Frederic Edwin Church (1858)

Contents

FIRST HALF: INTO THE WAR

SECOND HALF:
THE JOURNEY TO THE WORLD BELOW

Preface for Those with an
Aversion to "Theory"

This book is an attempt to understand Francis Ford Coppola's 1979 masterpiece *Apocalypse Now*–though I have given preference to the later 2001 version released as *Apocalypse Now Redux*–in terms of the basic conceptual vocabulary of what is known as "Critical Theory." That is, more or less, what postmodern–and now "hypermodern"–philosophy generally goes by these days and it is largely a creation of French theoreticians of the 1950s and 1960s–Lacan and Foucault were first on the mark here–responding to and translating the discourse of *two* crucially important German-speaking thinkers: Martin Heidegger and Ferdinand de Saussure (who was Swiss). Lacan's work, especially, is based on a synthesis of ideas borrowed from Sigmund Freud and hybridized with Saussurean linguistics, and it was Jean-Paul Sartre who introduced Heidegger to French audiences. Derrida is impossible to understand without him.

But for the general reader who regards all this as rubbish, yet still retains an interest in understanding the various "meanings" embedded in such a complex work of celluloid art as *Apocalypse Now*, a familiarity with these ideas is not *absolutely* necessary in order to read through the following work, which is written primarily with a general audience in mind. All one need do is simply to skip the book's Introduction (where most of its theoretical apparatus is located), and one or two paragraphs here and there in the main body of the text which invoke Lacan or Gadamer; the rest should be perfectly intelligible to him (or her, as the case may be) since, as my readers well know, I do not write in the private language of "academese." I have, however, structured my interpretation of the film as a kind of agon of Jung against Lacan–the reader can, if he (or she) wishes, think of me as a kind of "Anti-Zizek"–and for those wishing to know at least the basics of Lacan, I can recommend no better work than *An Introductory Dictionary of Lacanian Psychoanalysis* by Dylan Evans. There the reader can quickly and efficiently look up terms like "The Name of the Father," "the Phallus," "L-schema," etc. for precise and widely comprehensible definitions of Lacan's main ideas. I claim to be no master of Lacan, but he is one of the most important figures in the evolution of Critical Theory and *some* acquaintance with his ideas is necessary for understanding its point of view. One, for instance, simply cannot read Slavoj Zizek without some basic knowledge of Lacan.

But as I say, familiarity with Lacan–or even Jung–isn't, strictly speaking, necessary for reading through the present work, most of which is written for the average educated reader who is interested in unpacking the semiotics of *Apocalypse Now*.

Coppola's film, released in 1979, was *the* climactic work of the so-called "Film School Generation" that came out of Los Angeles and San Francisco in the 1970s. It simultaneously wrapped up and completed that epoch, while Coppola's protégé and later, rival, George Lucas, was busy inaugurating a *new* epoch of cinema with his 1977 classic film *Star Wars* (Lucas, of course, having been assigned as the original director for *Apocalypse Now*, though he passed on it in favor of *Star Wars* and handed it back to Coppola as the first film for his new production company American Zoetrope). *Star Wars* must be regarded not as climactic–in the sense in which ecologists speak of a "climax forest"–but rather as "formative" for an entirely new generation of special effects-based cinema that dominated the 1980s and much of the 1990s and which, in turn, achieved *its* climax with James Cameron's *Titanic* in 1997, marking the beginnings of the end of cinema's two-decade long apotheosis. From that point on, the medium became overburdened by its own technological innovations, and the switch from analogue to digital–beginning, appropriately, once again with a new *Star Wars* film, namely, *The Phantom Menace* in 1999–brought the whole majestic arc crashing down into the epoch of what I have termed "post-classic cinema": an age of recycled formulae, sequels, remakes and a general timidity regarding new ideas.[1]

Innovation has now been replaced by adulation of the "Old Masters," and an attempt to imitate them and their visionary styles, which currently predominates on the big screen. Hence, J.J. Abrams and his various endeavors to imitate both Spielberg and Lucas, or Zack Snyder, who patterns himself after John Carpenter, or even Christopher Nolan–probably the best of the bunch–with his following in the footsteps of James Cameron. Paul Thomas Anderson, with films like *There Will Be Blood* and *Inherent Vice*, has tried–and failed–to fill the shoes of Stanley Kubrick (while Terrence Malick, meanwhile–alone amongst them, a true genius–is a dinosaur left over from a previous age, when his career ran into difficulties and was put into hibernation for two decades). *The Tree of Life* is a masterpiece on par with anything produced by the Old Masters, but film nowadays, for the most part, is no longer capable of innovation and has become top-heavy with the weight of its own technological "accursed share."

Apocalypse Now was made back in the days when visionary directors, on fire with genius, and given free reign by studios to do as they liked–provided profits were still being made–could get away with taking the kinds of outrageous daredevil risks that

Coppola and, for instance, Werner Herzog were up to in those days (Herzog's *Fitzcarraldo*, released in 1982, was a kind of homage–whether consciously or not on Herzog's part–to *Apocalypse Now*). Trekking with cameras and big budgets out into the world's roughest jungles and barren deserts, however–and to return from those dark corners of the earth with largely analogue images–was a cultural cycle that was nearing its end by 1982, as a new kind of Spielberg-Lucas influenced special effects cinema–based on optical effects and matte paintings that looked fabulously convincing to the eye–was just getting off the ground.

Apocalypse Now is the "climax forest" of the 1970s American auteur development in Hollywood–under the aegis of the very hip producer Robert Evans–that was largely a response to the European auteurs of the French and Italian cinemas of the 1950s. If the Rolling Stones and the Beatles had been Europe's response to Elvis Presley and Johnny Cash, films like *Taxi Driver* and *The Godfather* were the American response to continental films like Godard's *Breathless* or Bernardo Bertolucci's *The Conformist*. It was a giddy and exciting decade for cinema because it seemed like absolutely *anything* was possible and one never knew what sorts of "dangerous images" lay just around the corner at the local theater.

But film is a dangerous art form no longer. It is now safe and cozy, directed at suburban SUV-driving families with soccer moms and kids riding ATVs up and down neatly manicured green-lawned streets. It is all designed to please, patronize, protect and coat life in the shopping mall suburbs with a thin plastic residue of sticky and comforting CGI images designed to reinforce the materialistic illusions that the American Way of Life is the Best.

Meanwhile, it has been left up to contemporary art to take over the "dangerous" role which film once occupied in our culture, and indeed, hypermodernity's best artists–of the caliber of

Damien Hirst, Odd Nerdrum or Anish Kapoor—are the imaginative ones busy creating dangerous and challenging images for those who want nothing to do with the middle class version of a safe and (once again) conformist American society dominated by MILFs.

Apocalypse Now was, and still is—as I hope to show in the following analysis—a *dangerous* film packed with adrenalized images and morally difficult ideas. While watching the movie as an eleven-year-old child for the first time, I can remember being simultaneously terrified and yet also thrilled by the film's complex and dream-like images. As I gaped at Coppola's narrative of the little PBR going up river towards a destination ever more and more saturated with images of madness and chaos, I grew nervous in my seat, and had no idea what sort of incredible image would hit me next and go resonating through my imagination for the next few weeks as I tried to sleep at night. That is the kind of power those images had back then. You didn't forget them for months after you were exposed to them. Film is simply no longer capable of this kind of avant-garde "shock of the new" anymore.

So, for now, let's take another look at them and see what kind of relevance they have to a globalized posthistoric society facing an uncertain future of endless terrorist wars and global warming.

Welcome (back) to a dangerous art form.

I hope you enjoy the tour.

Introduction by Way of an Answer to the Question, "How do *You* Know What the Artist Meant?"

Drawing an "X" Over Lacan

According to Lacan, we never *say* what we actually *mean*, since there are always other meanings tripping up our conscious intentions. The unconscious is always working at cross-purposes with what we think we want to say. (Hence, it follows that we also never know which "I" is speaking, for Lacan's conception of the Self is Cubist: it could be Mother that is speaking, or Father or a friend, etc.) The ego and the Subject, for him, are working at cross-purposes, for Lacan associates the ego with the Imaginary Order that begins with the Mirror Stage and the ego's first (false) identification of itself with a specular image (which, nevertheless, unifies the infant's hitherto fragmented body; hence, when in the beginning of *Apocalypse Now*, Willard shatters the image of himself in the mirror, he is regressing to that state of early infantile fragmentation).

It is important to emphasize that images, for Lacan, always get in the way and "trip up" the conscious ego. The Subject, on the other hand, the true Subject (for the ego is a fiction of the Subject) is identified with the Symbolic Order, not the Imaginary Order, and the Symbolic Order differs from the Imaginary

Order in that it is not made up of images with the potential to lead one astray–i.e. the biker revving up his motorcycle who thinks he's an image of Marlon Brando in *The Wild One*–but rather the Symbolic Order is made up of *linguistic* signifiers, signifiers be it said, that can actually get trapped in the body and produce neurotic symptoms. The Symbolic Order, furthermore, is the order of the Big Other–i.e. Freud's Superego–and in order to accede to it, there must take place on the part of the Subject a successful "castration."

A successful castration, according to Lacan, is necessary for the Subject to attain to proper signification in the Symbolic Order, otherwise, a psychosis may result. The individual child has to give up being the Phallus for the Mother, and in doing so, accedes to the paternal authority represented by the Name of the Father. Desire for the Mother, in other words, must give way to the Name of the Father (by letting go of trying to be the Phallus; hence "castration"), for if the Father is foreclosed–that is, if castration fails to take place–then the individual will not be able to function properly within the Symbolic Order of society and may become psychotic.

Lacan's thinking, then, is tantamount to a "crossing out" of the ego's identification with the specular images and phantasms of the imaginary order and building a kind of wall made out of linguistic signifiers that ruptures it by connecting the Subject properly with the Big Other. This is Lacan's famous L-schema, wherein is diagrammed this "crossing out" of the ego's identification with the various specular images with which it mistakes itself.[2] For Lacan–as for Freud before him–the order of the Father is *supremely* spiritual and he therefore de-privileges that of the Mother, which he associates with the realm of images, myths and dreams, or "phantasms" in other words.[3]

It was one of Deleuze's major projects, however, to "counter" Lacan–hence the title of his and Guattari's book *Anti-Oedipus* really refers to a stance taken up in *opposition* not so much to Freud as to Lacan[4]–and so in his book *Masochism*, Deleuze insisted that though sado-masochism is always thought of as a single complex, the two components–sadism and masochism–are actually quite different phenomena. For whereas sadism is associated with the order of the Father, who is always doing cruel things to his children, masochism is all about a contract that is made with the Mother in order to *exclude* the Father from the Symbolic Order. It is, therefore, a reversal of Lacanian castration in favor of Bachofen's order of Mother Right that he had discovered in his 1861 book *Das Mutterrecht*.[5]

How all this is relevant to *Apocalypse Now* will be demonstrated shortly, but for the time being we will just say that my reading of the film is all about an alliance made with the Mother to recover the Imaginary Order of myth, dream and zodiac, and to *expel* the paternal authority of the Father (i.e. the US Army) from Willard's symbolic order. It is tantamount to the drawing of a gigantic "X" over Lacan's L-schema in favor of a more Jungian approach to the semiotics of the psyche.

The Textual Unconscious

But Lacan's point, which we started with, still stands: we never *say* exactly what we *mean* because the unconscious is like a cloud of *other* signifiers that are always tripping up our intended meanings. The same goes for artists: they never *say* exactly what they *think* they mean because their works are packed with so many other unintended meanings, that we may as well say that each text, work of art, etc. comes equipped with its own unconscious. Hence, the task of the cultural critic is to act as a sort of psychoanalyst of culture. His job is to make the *unintended* meanings in the work of art visible. He is a fisherman of signifiers, in other words. But how good of a job he does in this operation depends on the quality of the tools used. The wrong bait may attract the wrong fish.

I have approached the "meanings" in *Apocalypse Now* on two other occasions in my career as a cultural critic: once for a series of YouTube videos that I did on the semiotics of various films—and the critique of *Apocalypse Now* consisted of a videotape commentary that I made circa 1996 that I then later uploaded to You-Tube circa 2006 or so—and once as an early essay (a fake interview, actually) in my second book, the 2005 work entitled *Celluloid Heroes, Mechanical Dragons*.[6] Over the years, I have noticed a tendency for people to object to the interpretations with the question: "Yes, but how could Coppola have known that?" etc. etc., and my response with the present work is precisely to invoke Lacan's idea that since we never *say* exactly what we *mean*, then neither does the artist. Each work therefore comes to us with its own textual unconscious that is packed full of signifiers which have escaped the artist's conscious intentions. But that doesn't mean they aren't still there, like Derridean traces, surrounding the work with a logospheric cloud of possible meanings.

In a similar fashion, when Heidegger wrote his famous essay on "The Essence of Truth,"[7] he maintained that for every stance that is consciously taken, other aspects of an entity withdraw into concealment and fall off the radar. As entities unconceal themselves, that is to say, they function like Hyperobjects[8]: there is always an infinitely larger number of facets to them than we can ever fully grasp at once because for each aspect of an entity that unconceals itself in the truth Clearing, all its other facets withdraw into concealment.

Likewise with the artist and his work of art. The cultural critic's task is to illuminate those aspects of a work that have withdrawn into the *Abgrund* of concealment. He participates in the Clearing—which is simply the space of encounter between entities in a cultural horizon—by unconcealing lost, repressed or forgotten "traces" from the subducted "meaning cloud" that hides implicitly within each work of art.

Gadamer, in his *Truth and Method*, on the other hand, makes a distinction between the text per se and the work of art: the text—and presumably he means works like Thucydides's *History of the Pelopennesian War* or Aeschylus's *Oresteia*—does not exist per se; it is like the Kantian thing-in-itself that is forever beyond our reach precisely because we can only see those aspects of it with the tools of the *a priori* concepts that are built into the very structure of our Understanding. The object as it is in itself is forever unknowable. Likewise, Gadamer's theory of the text tells us that the text-in-itself is unreachable precisely because we are embedded in specific ages with particular biases that structure how we "read" a particular work. Each age therefore constructs the text anew as relevant for its own age.[9] Today's reading of Aeschylus's *Oresteia* could not possibly resemble the original intentions of the Greeks because their cultural horizon has long since ceased to function and we can only make guesses at what we thought they meant. Hence, for Gadamer there *is* no text-in-itself.

But the work of art, on the other hand—and presumably Gadamer meant things like specific art objects, sculptures, paintings, etc.—is a kind of emanation of an age's particular understanding of Being. It is an avatar of Being, for that age, and therefore actually *gains* Being as it takes the perceiving subject into its feedback loop and includes him therein.[10] The text, on the other hand, *loses* Being as it recedes from his grasp.

For Derrida, though, the text is the *only* thing that counts, since, in the absence of transcendental signifieds, texts simply refer to each other in an infinite process of sliding signification which he calls "differance." There are only texts-within-texts to infinity, since each text is composed of other texts which have been "folded" into one another like origami, containing citations of utterances that have been surgically removed from one context and placed into another as a fresh "iteration" of that utterance whose meanings are changed by the placement into a differing– and deferring–context.[11]

So, whereas for Gadamer the text-in-itself has receded from our grasp and dissolved into a kind of phantom particle wave function of diffuse potential meanings, for Derrida the text lights up and *gains* being precisely because it is a unique construct composed out of an infinite tissue of meanings that hover about it in trace clouds of unauthorized signifiers that were repressed during the Logocentric Age, when only *one* meaning of each binarity– writing vs. the voice, let's say–was privileged, while the other was repressed into the textual unconscious.

My present reading of *Apocalypse Now*–which is based on the 2001 long version of the film known as *Apocalypse Now Redux*– differs greatly from my two earlier readings, but it does not anathematize them, any more than one critic's reading of a text anathematizes all others. The point I have been making here is that the meaning clouds of repressed signifiers surrounding each text or work of art are *infinite*, and what the critic manages to fish out of the meaning reservoir depends on what tools he / she used when he / she went diving down in there. For my early readings, I used only the comparative mythology of Jung and his disciples Joseph Campbell, Erich Neumann, etc. For the present reading, I have used the tools of contemporary critical theory. Different tools fish up different kinds of animals.

What I am "Against"

According to the contemporary Greek philosopher Corne- lius Castoriadis, Heidegger's reduction of the history of philoso- phy to the history of Being crushes the essence of philosophy as debate. Heidegger's reduction, for Castoriadis, was tantamount to a silencing of the Greek tradition of debate through *polemos* and *agon*, since it reduces every philosopher to the same onto-logical status as every other: all have forgotten "being." The po-lemical strife that is the essence of the Greek philosophical *agon* is therefore completely *missing* from Heidegger who ends up in-advertently silencing the Greek tradition of agonic debate and polemic strife.[12]

Thus, if Derrida–who comes from an Algerian-Jewish back-ground–attacks Western logocentrism through deconstruction as a kind of continuation of the Maccabean Revolt by other means, Castoriadis tries to retrieve the Greek polis and plant it right in the middle of our consumer ecumene (just as Heidegger, consistent with Germanic historical thinking, transforms philos-ophy into the *history* of philosophy). Every society, Castoriadis insists, is guided by what he termed "imaginary significations" that function as ruling *archai* guiding that society: Hebrew laws, Greek gods, etc.[13] The social imaginaries of traditional societ-ies are "heteronomous," in the sense that their significations are pre-given and closed for all time, unless they are ruptured by an act of what Catoriadis calls "philosophical autonomy." This has only happened, for Castoriadis, twice in the West: in Athens dur-ing the fifth century, and in modern philosophy beginning with Descartes. The task of philosophy is to teach the individual to become autonomous: not to ask, what is Being? but rather, what do *I* think about being, justice, *physis*, etc.

In the consumer society, meaning has closed down once again into mediatized consensus and political apathy. The only ruling *archai* are those that pertain to the consumer ethos to shop, buy and spend. All other incentives for the individual to become critical of social institutions have disappeared.[14]

With the philosophical agon of Castoriadis in mind, then, I wish to offer my reading of *Apocalypse Now against* a certain strain of posthistoric thinking: for I side with Sloterdijk *against* Zizek; with Deleuze & Guattari *against* Lacan; and with Jung *against*

Freud. All of these thinkers, though brilliant, have brought into contemporary philosophy a scathing contempt of myth, ritual and symbol, identifying them as part of the ontologically injurious baggage left over from the metaphysical age. Even Rene Girard, who alone among them has any real grasp of myth, does so only from the point of view of the official doctrine of Freud.

Hence, in the debate over myth that began with Freud *against* Jung, I am siding, quite consciously with Jung here, despite all his faults.

But I am going to do this by fishing into the textual unconscious of *Apocalypse Now* to find what I believe its ruling *archai*, or imaginary significations, to be.

Those *archai*, I will insist, are quite consistent with Castoriadis's philosophy of the attainment of a critical stance of autonomy that empowers the individual to stand on his own and think for himself *against* institutions like those of the US military megamachine.

Captain Willard has a long journey ahead of him.

Let's get to it, shall we?

FIRST HALF:
INTO THE WAR

(0:00:00 - 0:07:30)
Willard's Self-Destruction

As *Apocalypse Now* opens, we begin with "the end."

The inceptual image of the film is that of a wall of dark green palm trees with pale brown trunks entangled densely together; so densely, in fact, as to suggest a natural barrier of some sort, a wall that must be broken, ruptured and blown apart to allow the process of signification to take place. And indeed, just as the voice of Jim Morrison announces on the film's soundtrack, "This is the end," the tree line simultaneously explodes into crimson flames as it is bombed from an airstrike that will occur later on in the film, during its famous "Kilgore" episode (the scene is a flash forward from that sequence). Helicopters cut through the air in one or two slow motion passes in front of the camera, like enormous gray-green prehistoric dragonflies.

For the first seven minutes of the film, in lieu of a title sequence, Coppola orchestrates a montage depicting the main character Willard in a self-destructive mode inside of a brown-and-vanilla-walled apartment room in Saigon. (Michael Herr—the author of Willard's voice-over narration—in the very first chapter of his *Dispatches*, complains of depressions whenever he was back in Saigon).[15] The various signifiers on Willard's nightstand lay out the path of destruction that is already in *medias res* as the film opens: a pair of dogtags, a splayed wallet looking gutted; a pack of cigarettes with a silver Zippo lighter on top, a bottle of Martinelli Cordon Bleu liquor, letters from Willard's wife,

29

her black and white photograph, and the gun that he keeps near his pillow, indicating that he has been thinking about suicide.

The camera's point of view from above looking downward at Willard, furthermore, as he sits cross-legged on the floor of the tiny, stale room, emphasizes the suffocating feeling of the walls closing in on him as he goes stir crazy, surrounded by the various derelict shells of his own self-destruction: cups, bowls, empty liquor bottles, discarded bits of trash and stained pages of damp, disused newspaper.

The song that plays on the soundtrack, meanwhile, "The End," was originally written– according to Jim Morrison–in 1967 about the end of a relationship with a girlfriend: and as Willard's voice-over narration makes clear, his own marriage has indeed ended. He carefully sears her photograph with a cigarette dangling from his mouth while lying in bed, as though to make the point.

But this is also a man who has reached the end of his rope, as a process of Cornelius Castoriadis has termed "significative closure," in which all lines of meaning connecting the individual to his particular social formation have been severed. What Castoriadis had in mind was the idea that traditional societies are what he termed "heteronomous," in the sense that their social imaginary significations are "closed" once and for all, and that the "autonomous rupture" which it is the task of philosophy to undertake has only opened them up, as I stated in the Introduction, twice in history with innovative thinking: once in fifth century Athens, and once during the age of Modernity from Descartes down to about 1950 when, with the rise of the consumer society and the death of both (true) democracy and philosophy, "significative closure" occurred once again. In the post WWII society, according to Castoriadis, there are only a few anthropological types left available for the individual to effectuate, and that of the consumer is paramount. The consumer is one who is "consensisized" into the capitalist ideology in a manner that encourages him *not* to think for himself or become "autonomous," but simply rather to conform and follow the meaning lines laid down by the capitalist ideology of media advertising, billboards, magazines, commercials, and television shows. This, in turn, robs him of the ability to use critical thinking to challenge the state and media apparatus in the Greek tradition of *polemos* and *agon,* or the strife that produces fresh ideas through challenging the norm.[16]

In Willard's case, an analogous event of "significative closure" has occurred in his own life, for he is surrounded by walls and emotional barricades that have cut him off from all macrolines of meaning that would plug him into a functioning social multiplicity. He is in a box, in other words, cut off from relations with society and indeed Lacan's entire symbolic order of the Big Other and all that goes along with it, which has totally receded from his grasp.

The bombing of the wall of the palm tree line, however—the equivalent of what the contemporary poet Michael Aaron Kamins calls "this palmtime deathline"[17]—suggests the possibility of the occurrence of a rupture of closure and the attainment by Willard of an autonomous stance that will activate the process of signification for him once again. And indeed, the journey that he is about to undertake—a journey that will carry him beyond that tree line into the far depths of the *Abgrund* that it contains—will reactivate meaning for him, as he sets off in quest of a new anthropological type that will unplug him from the paternal authority of the military order and create that type of autonomous thinking which Castoriadis had in mind, a thinking in which he will be able to stand on his own, for himself, as an Individual unplugged from the social codes of the military that has captured and constrained his life to fit into its molar lines.

In order to do this, however, he will require a confrontation with the Other–Colonel Walter E. Kurtz, as it turns out–who will provide him with an alternative model to the symbolic order of the paternal authority that hence far, Willard has operated *on the inside of* as an assassin working for the US Army. (By this point, he has already assassinated six people; note that Kurtz will be his seventh, implying the completion of a cycle).

To put it in the terms of Lacanian discourse, then, by the film's conclusion, he will come unplugged from the Name of the Father and–in an alliance with the Mother (and here the so-called French Plantation Scene, cut from the original theatrical release, will prove essential)–he will enter into an imaginary order that is entirely autonomous and subverts all paternal authority. He will, in effect, destroy Lacan's symbolic order–and especially its "L-schema"–precisely by recovering the lost (Jungian) imaginary of image, myth and zodiac, thereby *reversing* Lacanian castration and subverting its order with another one altogether. He will rediscover the lost Phallus when he picks up the machete at the film's conclusion and uses it to kill Kurtz.

Hence, another significance of the song playing over the film's opening montage, for its lyrics famously refer to a man who kills his father and "fucks" his mother. This is the rupturing of the paternal metaphor and its disassemblage and recoding into the order of the mother, wherein one's true *Abgrund* rests. The process is similar to the way in which Deleuze, in his book on *Masochism*, turns Oedipus upside down by demonstrating that masochism, as an entirely separate phenomenon from sadism, is all about a contract made with the Mother to keep the Father *out* of the symbolic order, and to reconstruct an imaginary based on Bachofen's Mother Right.[18] The foreclosure of the Name of the Father does not *necessarily* lead to psychosis: in Willard's case, it will lead him to the "autonomous rupture" of Castoriadis, wherein an opportunity for new meaning will irrupt into his life precisely by unplugging him from the paternal order.

Note also that the lyrics of "The End," (which is a 12 minute song that cuts off in the opening montage after only a few minutes and so this part is not audible on the film's soundtrack) contain the image of riding on the back of a snake: "ride the snake / to the lake, the ancient lake, baby / the snake is long, seven miles." The snake is, of course, the river that will carry Willard and his crew into the heart of darkness in Cambodia, but it is also evocative of the myth of the Chinese dragon which carries the souls of the dead on its back into the celestial heavens. And since the dragon, in Chinese myth, inevitably forms a dual signifier with the Tiger–the Tiger is West, the Dragon is East–the song also contains the missing half of the binarity that will later in the film be supplemented by the encounter with the tiger in the jungle when the crew stop for a break in a cool mangrove clearing.

And let us not forget that the wall of palm trees also suggests the various Great Walls with which civilizations in their "end times" bound themselves in, erecting barriers against the external proletariat barbarians that lie yonder and which pose a threat to the very nature of the civilized order itself. "The End" suggests the end phases of great civilizations which inevitably cycle down into the creation of Universal States built on erecting walls and colonizing the "dark lands" of the Cultural Other: the Gauls, for instance, or the Vandals of North Africa, or Spain, etc. etc. Hence, the US endeavor in Vietnam invites comparison with the campaigns of a Caesar in the forests of Gaul, or a Pompey in the deserts of Spain, building vast new colonialist annexes to add to their crumbling empires (Colonel Kilgore fits this role especially well). This is a film, Coppola suggests, about the neo-Roman empire of the American Universal State that is venturing beyond the pale into zones of cultural Otherness that it knows nothing about and does not understand.

"The End," furthermore, is also obviously apocalyptic: it suggests the advent of a Kali Yuga, or an age of the world's darkening, as Heidegger once put it,[19] in which beings have been abandoned by Being and the gods have withdrawn into concealment. The kinds of moral chaos and depravity which follow such abandonments go very, very far back in ancient literature, indeed, as far back as the Sumerian poem known as "The Curse of Akkad" (written circa. 2100 BC) in which the destruction of the city of Akkad by invasions from Gutian barbarians is portrayed as the result of the city's patron goddess Inanna withdrawing her favors from the city and abandoning it.[20] Thus, Heidegger's concept of the contemporary withdrawal of the gods did not originate with either him or Holderlin, but has a *very* ancient pedigree. The Chinese too knew this tradition, which they called "the withdrawal of the Mandate of Heaven," which every new dynasty invoked to justify the shift from one to the other; from, say, the Shang to the Chou Dynasties, implying a prior moral depravity in the preceding age which the new dynasty was divinely appointed to fix.

And indeed, Coppola's three hour and sixteen minute opus will carry us on a journey–riding on the back of the water snake– through the morally depraved and directionally disorienting Vietnam War, a landscape full of "hollow men" and wasted lands.

(0:07:30 - 0:09:16)
Summons

In this sequence, two military men climb the shadowy staircase to Willard's apartment in order to bring him the summons to Nha Trang, where he will be given his mission to kill Colonel Walter E. Kurtz. Willard is bloody from having cut his hand while striking and shattering the mirror on the previous evening–indicating his ego's current dissatisfaction with its specular image as a military assassin–and he is intensely hung over. He also assumes that, like K. at the beginning of Kafka's novel *The Trial*, in which two men show up in K.'s apartment to inform him of his seizure by the state, that he is under arrest and asks what the charges are. But it is only a summons to an adventure that he is not currently prepared for, and so he must be dragged, against his will, into the shower. Though he is in a state of maximum spiritual entropy, the shower has the effect of "waking him up," for it wrings a scream out of him, like a newborn baby emerging from its mother's birth canal.

This "baptism" should be contrasted with the one that occurs near the end of the film, when Kurtz's Montagnard army baptize Willard by dragging him through the rain and wet mud of the earth. Whereas the current scene is a military baptism by water that appropriates the elements of the traditional Christian baptism–which has the effect of incorporating the individual into the paternal order of the Church–the later baptism near the film's conclusion is a baptism that undoes the military overcoding of paternal authority and replaces it with the authority of

Mother Earth. It is analogous to the "earth-touching" mudra of the Buddha, who reaches out to touch Mother Earth in order to invoke her as a "witness" to his enlightenment just as the morning star is rising. Kurtz's order, too, is based on a line of flight that he has traced in order to escape the codes of the military sign regime, in an alliance with the (feminine) codes of the jungle, the earth, and the various local goddesses of the Montagnards.

For now, Willard's mission is given to him as an overcoding by the military sign regime, in which he will be rendered capable of being plugged into the various military assemblages of man-plus-machine: that is to say, man-plus-helicopter, man-plus-boat, man-plus-gun, etc. These are all paternal assemblages and they are in alliance with the codes given to him under the Name of the Father.

(0:09:17 - 0:18:50)
The Mission

In this scene, Willard is given his mission to proceed up the
Nung River and "terminate the command" of Colonel Walter E.
Kurtz, a Green Beret colonel who has apparently gone insane and
gives orders to his own private army of Montagnard troops who
carry out any of those orders, "however ridiculous." The military
officials play a tape recording of Kurtz, in which he expounds
upon watching a "snail crawl along the edge of a straight razor,"
and claims that it is his dream, his nightmare, this "crawling and
slithering." The military officials, all sitting down with Willard in
a kind of Last Supper, emphasize that Kurtz is out there "beyond
the pale" still in the field "commanding troops," and that he has
gone *totally* insane. Willard agrees with this assessment and takes
the cigarette that is offered to him, while he is told to terminate
the colonel's command "with extreme prejudice."

Kurtz, in other words, has become totally "autonomous,"
operating on his own without authorization by the military and
commanding his own private army. The *real* reason the military
wants him dead is to crush out this autonomy: he is not following the lines of overcoding laid down upon him through years
of specialized military training, and has instead, broken free of
the military apparatus of control and traced a line of flight into
the jungle, where he has destratified from the plane of military
organization to set up his own kingdom. The story reminds one
of Werner Herzog's 1972 film *Aguirre: the Wrath of God*, which
tells the tale of the first mad conquistador to declare indepen-

dence from the Spanish crown and to set up his own kingdom in the South American jungles. Just as that story ended in madness and destruction, so too, Coppola implies, will Kurtz's.

But for Kurtz, as we will see, the military that created him is tantamount to a tyranny in which all meanings are closed because they are pre-given, and the individual is thus disempowered to use his own critical thinking to rupture that closure and allow the creation of new significations to occur. Kurtz will teach Willard how to think for himself, and it is this encounter with the Other that will transform him and set him free from the specular image–in the mirror that he had shattered–of being an army assassin, and hence a mere pawn in the larger game of global politics. (Note that this is the very *opposite* of what happens in the recent 2014 film *American Sniper,* in which the American assassin Chris Kyle is celebrated precisely for conforming, in an uncritical manner, with his role as a pawn in the creation of the American Empire).

Of course, the question of military commanders breaking free from their authorized codes and creating their own private armies is not a new one: it is precisely what Julius Caesar did when he became rich enough, through selling slaves captured in Gaul, to afford to pay his own troops, who thus transferred their loyalty to *him*, instead of to Rome (thereby paving the way for the Civil Wars). The same went for Pompey, his enemy on the battlefield at Pharsalus, who was rich enough to afford his own private army from acquiring real estate (Pompey's conquests, by contrast, were mostly in Spain). And Crassus, attempting to imitate his two rivals of the First Triumvirate–he was richer than both, but far less popular–set out for the Middle East in a ludicrous attempt to imitate Alexander the Great by going on a campaign to rid Palestine of the Parthian menace, fully equipped with his own private army. He had intended to carry this campaign all the way to India, just like Alexander. Crassus, however, did not fare as well, for he and his troops were *badly* beaten by the Parthian bowmen and his head ended up being paraded on a stick by the Parthian commander, whose military skills Crassus had vastly underestimated. And then, with his sudden disappearance from the Triumvirate, the way was cleared for Caesar and Pompey to fight it out amongst themselves until Caesar was the last man standing and the Roman Empire was on the way to its completion.

It is, then, one of the structural dangers of the days of Empire and Universal States: the generals may become so powerful that they break off to form their own lines of flight with their own private armies. This is an issue, furthermore, that has particular relevance to the problem of today's so-called PMC's, or private military companies, such as Blackwater or Aegis Defense Services, which are normally composed of ex-soldiers who give their loyalty not to any state Constitution, but to the highest bidder, a bidder who often turns out to be a private entrepeneur. One can only guess, then, what the outcome of such ominous developments will be when state coups utilizing such hired mercenaries become more and more common.[21]

But the other interesting thing about this scene is that it introduces us, subliminally, to the *Apocalypse Now* bestiary (subliminally because the animal signifiers are all in the backgrounds of the shots and are not noticed until after many viewings): the room inside the military trailer is furnished with animal signifiers everywhere. On the walls, there are mounted antelope heads; in the glass case behind the seated military leaders are ceramic elephants; and on the wall above Harrison Ford's head (a character who name tag is "Lucas"), when Willard first walks into the trailer, there appears to be what looks like a flying horse, an allusion to the Air-Cav sequence with Kilgore that will soon follow. The roast beef that is served during the briefing also looks ahead to the slaughter of the water buffalo at the film's climax (which is actually Kurtz in theriomorphic form, making this supper a kind of sacramental "eating" of him), and the basket of shrimp that is passed around weirdly echoes the recording of Kurtz talking about a snail crawling along the edge of a straight razor.

The bestiary of *Apocalypse Now* is large and it is hugely important for understanding the film's signifiers: from the flying horses of the Air-Cav to the "rabbit" of the Playboy bunnies, and onward to the birds, the tiger, the bull, etc., *Apocalypse Now* is packed with theriomorphic symbols which help provide clues to unlocking the film's codes, as we shall see.

There is already a suggestion in this sequence inside the trailer–and this is especially evident with Kurtz's description of the snail–of devolution and regression to the status of a becoming-animal that will form one of the film's major motifs. Regression to one's most brutal, zoological animal instincts is never very far behind any of the characters as they chart their course across the film's topological landscape, for regression and devolution to baser and more primordial animalistic forms–together with the moral depravity that results–is one of the film's main ideas. Indeed, it is as though the film were tracing the history of religious iconology in reverse: from the human gods of Christianity, to the mainly human deities–some occasionally half-animal, like the centaurs–of the Greeks; and back, further, to the African bestiary of the gods of ancient Egypt, in which theriomorphic gods dominated, and managed to hold, the stage of religious evolution for two thousand years. The journey backward–or perhaps "devolution" is better–to an increase in theriomorphic signifiers in the religious pantheon also tends to increase the effects of what Jean Gebser termed the "magical consciousness structure," that primordial religious consciousness of aboriginal and tribal man (where Coppola's film ends up).[22]

(0:18:50 - 0:20:17)
Bird / Snake

The transition to the next shot takes place as the camera melts through the curtains of the trailer to an expansive, wide-angled view of Willard being carried via helicopter to the Nung River. The topological landscape of Vietnam is shown with undulating hills far beneath the lone helicopter, and, as Willard's voice-over explains how he decided to take the mission because he had no idea what else to do—otherwise it would be back to the self-destruction inside his Saigon apartment—the mode of transportation in the dromosphere shifts from helicopter to Navy Patrol Boat (PBR for short) as it fuels up at the local Texaco station along the river. Willard tells us that he has already assassinated six people, but never an officer and never an American, and that this is causing him some anxiety. (The successful completion of his assassination of Kurtz will bring him to the top, as it were, of the ancient seven storey mountain).

The mythic substructures—if we may "psychologize" here (borrowing James Hillman's term from *Revisioning Psychology* in which concepts and images are "seen through" to their archetypal endo-skeletons)[23]—of the gods in these machines are: the viewpoint, first, of a mechanical flying Garuda bird, the great mythical solar bird that carries the god Vishnu on its back in Indian mythology; and second, as the camera's point of view comes down to the river, the perspective of the *naga* or serpent is attained in the winding form of the Nung River itself.

The opposition between the solar Garuda bird and the lunar *naga* snakes in Indian myth visualizes in pictorial form the heat of the Indian sub-continent that scorches and dries up the waters of rivers, nightly dew, and wells and valleys. It also suggests the opposition between what Hillman termed "peaks" and "vales," or spirit and soul, an opposition that we will find recurring throughout the film.

For now, we are at the beginnings of a bird / snake opposition that plays in counterpoint as the film unfolds, as part of its zoological bestiary, along with its various codes. In the next sequence, this will be confirmed when the camera pans past Chef's arm on the patrol boat to reveal that he has a cobra tattooed on it, the shape of which recursively imitates the various windings of the Nung River which the PBR travels along, as well as Coppola's very loosely plotted narrative structure that meanders and winds its way along in serpentine fashion.

This kind of narrative structure, by the way, in which whole scenes can be added or deleted or even shifted around without detriment to the point of the narrative is a very old one, going all the way back to the ancient Homeric epics sung by the bards. The work of Albert B. Lord[24] has shown us that such singers can remove or add whole episodes to their narratives at will, and undoubtedly the pre-literate bards who sang *The Iliad* and *The Odyssey* did exactly that, for as Caroline Alexander has shown, the character of Achilles seems to have been a late addition to *The Iliad*, since most of the story unfolds without his presence in it, and he has some characteristics–being the youngest of the warriors, for instance–that mark him off as a very different character from the others.[25]

As Walter Ong, furthermore, has pointed out, the first tightly plotted narratives in Western literature were the Greek tragedies which differed from the earlier epics in that they were written down from their inception.[26] They are products of a "literate" mentality, as Ong puts it, whereas the epics were "oral" in origin. Coppola, with his sprawling narrative, is merely retrieving this oral / epic tribal literary structure in which one can prefer the original 1979 short version, or the 2001 long version, which is the text that I am working on with this book. Recall, likewise, the various literary debates regarding *Hamlet*, which, when produced literally, is approximately four hours long, but scenes are routinely excised and moved around to create shorter versions, such as Franco Zeffirelli's 1990 *Hamlet* with Mel Gibson. Shakespeare's narrative, like Coppola's, still retains what Ong would call an "oral residue."

(0:20:18 - 0:24:04)
Introduction of the Crew

In this scene, which lasts approximately four minutes, Willard introduces us to the crew of his miniature *Argo*. In Jungian terms, it is important to note that, in addition to Willard there are precisely "four" crewmembers, which corresponds to Jung's idea that the ego has four functions: a thinking, feeling, sensation and intuitive function. Chef, the machinist, who also happens to be in training for cooking school, corresponds to the sensation function; while Lance, the surfer from California who always has sentimental attitudes corresponds to the feeling function. The Chief, a.k.a. Phillips, corresponds to the intuitive function, since he is the one who finds the way across difficult topological terrain and is always sensing the dangers of what lies ahead; while Willard himself would have to correspond to the thinking function, since he is the only one who "thinks" his way through the film as he sifts through the various dossiers that are given to him by Army Intelligence.

That leaves Clean, at 17 years old, the youngest crewmember, in the role of a sort of fifth, or Transcendent Function, who represents the *puer* archetype.

In terms, then, of the ancient doctrine of the four elements, Chef, the machinist and saucier, is in the role of earth; Lance, the surfer, corresponds to water; Phillips, with his combustive temperament, to fire; and Willard, the thinking man, to air. Clean, as his name implies, would then correspond to "ether" or the "quintessence," (fifth essence), the mercurial child who is put through the transformational processes of death and rebirth.

The semiotics of their various deaths, then, are interesting to consider as retrograde (to borrow from astrology) signifiers, for Clean is buried in the earth (Chef's element), while Phillips is carefully sent to a watery grave by Lance (hence, water putting out the Chief's fire once and for all); while Chef's beheading near the end of the film is a kind of death by air (the separation, that is, of the brain from the lungs: hence, no oxygen). Only Lance, the watery element, and Willard, the air (both have opposite valencies in the cosmology of the ancients: while water goes down and spreads, air rises up and spreads [fire simply goes up and earth goes down]), only Lance and Willard, that is to say, are left alive at the film's completion.

This is, of course, a Jungian reading, but I think it is important to consider in light of the fact that the film's semiotics are based upon an *undoing* of the paternal order of Lacan, with *his* mandala of the Self as the classic L-schema: Willard's ego, with its shattered identification with the specular image in the mirror creates an imaginary axis that "crosses" the proper axis of the Subject's attempt to relate to the Big Other (for Lacan, the ego is a "fiction" of the Subject). In Lacanian discourse, then, Freud's notion of "where Id was, there ego shall be" becomes: "where the imaginary order was, there the symbolic (i.e. language) will replace it," for the Subject's relation to the Big Other is the symbolic axis that *crosses* the ego's relation to the specular image that it has mistaken for itself. Lacan does not trust images, for in his theoretical universe, images are phantasmatic illusions that get in the way of the Subject's proper relation to the Big Other of society. The goal of Lacanian analysis is therefore to *break* the ego's identification with various "little others" that function as illusory replacements (*objets petit a*) for the long lost Phallus, and substitute that identification with a strong Subject relationship to the

46

Big Other of society. For this to happen, it is essential that the Subject's castration be successful and desire for the mother given up in place of accession to the Name of the Father, so that proper "signification," rather than psychosis, may take place. Lacan, however, believed that the Father belonged to a reality that is sacred in itself, "more spiritual," as he put it, "than any other." Following Freud, then, Lacan's order is patriarchal and anyone who deviates from the symbolic realm by misidentifying the ego with phantom self-images is "crossing" or blocking the Subject's relation to the Big Other and thereby preventing proper signification from taking place.

All of this, in Coppola's narrative, is being junked, for, as we will see, Willard shifts alliances from the paternal authority of the military to that of a secret compact with the Mother (during the French Plantation Scene) in which the Father is (ultimately) driven out from Willard's symbolic order, exactly as in Deleuze's theory of masochism. (Willard, that is, switches, in bi-polar fashion, from a manic mode when he is out hunting his prey–hence the sadistic component of his personality–to a depressive and self-destructive mode in between these episodes, hence the masochistic element. The film begins when he is in a masochistic mode in between assassinations).

Willard is the introverted thinking type who allows us access to the inside of his mind and what he is thinking as he sifts through, and analyzes–in the present scene–the first dossier on the life of Colonel Kurtz. He tells us, in voice-over narration, that it is an enigma to him why the military would want Kurtz dead because his career has been so exceptional. Kurtz, in other words, has slowly risen *upwards* throughout the course of his career, rising ever higher as he is decorated with more and more honors. Precisely when his "fall" took place is, at this point in the narrative, a mystery. Willard has just begun to contemplate why Kurtz decided at such a late age–"38 years old: why the fuck would he do that?" as he puts it—to join Airborne, when the scene transitions to the sounds of a Huey gun battle, thus shifting our point of view once again from the ground to the sky (or, in Hillman's terms, from the "vale" of the soul's interiority to the "peak" of the outer spiritual order).

Kilgore I

The crew hears a series of distant explosions and sees, on the horizon, a swarm of Hueys hovering and landing around the sooty smoke of a burning village which the Air-Cav has just destroyed. As they apprehensively pull their boat into the shoreline, tanks are still spewing flamethrowers in the background as the uprooted population of the village is being gathered up and herded off to other locations. The crew then disembark amidst the chaos, while Coppola turns up in a cameo, yelling at the disoriented men to "just go by like you're fighting!," as he is shooting a television documentary on the war. They are then warned that the C.O. ("commanding officer") is coming down in a chopper with the words "Death from Above" printed on its nose cone (Kilgore's chopper descends operatically, like the Queen of the Night in Mozart's *Magic Flute*). Lt. Col. Kilgore then climbs down out of the helicopter while the camera shoots him from below looking *up* in order to establish his mythic status as a giant.

Captain Willard then informs Kilgore that the Air-Cav was supposed to have been notified by II Corps that they were to provide the gunboat with an escort to the mouth of the Nung River, but Kilgore professes to know nothing about the communication and tells Willard to stay out of the way while he goes about systematically throwing "death cards" from a pack of traditional playing cards at dead bodies in order to, as Willard explains to Lance, "let Charlie know who did this." Kilgore's interest in Willard's mission then perks up when he is introduced to Lance

Johnson, a famous surfer from California whom Kilgore—a surfing fanatic—recognizes and immediately treats as a celebrity.

Near the ruins of a bombed-out cathedral, a helicopter can be seen airlifting cattle from a pen—presumably to be slaughtered and eaten for their beach barbecue in the next scene—while a priest performs mass before a small group of soldiers. Behind him, instead of the Crucified Redeemer, a tank blows hot oily flames upon some structure which withers beneath its onslaught, and the shot ends with a helicopter airlifting more cattle, in homage to the opening scene of *La Dolce Vita*, in which a helicopter carries a crucifix over the rooftops of a black and white Rome. (Behind the icon of Christ as the sacrificed one, in other words, there looms the much older "Tauroctony" of the slain bull, a central rite that was scattered throughout the religions of the Roman world ecumene in cults like Mithraism, the worship of Attis, the slaying of the Apis bull, etc). Hence, Coppola, in his film, is always concerned with giving us a "genealogy" of religious images and icons.

After this scene there follows a nighttime beach barbecue in which plans are made to airlift Willard's boat to the mouth of the Nung River, where a certain heavily-armed village must first be destroyed, although Colonel Kilgore is more excited by the possibilities of surfing the "six foot peak" that is located near the village than anything else. He is warned by his soldiers that the village is dangerous to Air-Cav because of its heavy ordinates and that it is known as "Charlie's Point," but Kilgore waves his hand dismissively at the apparently simple task of destroying the village as he comments, pointedly: "Charlie don't surf!"

The essence of the two scenes, then, is to introduce the viewer to the phenomenon of Lieutenant Colonel Kilgore as a larger than life figure of iconic status, which Coppola does by retrieving an ancient Old World aesthetic in which figures of spiritual importance are separated off into their own spaces, where they

Narmer Palette ~3000BCE

loom larger than any other figure in the composition, such as in the case of the Narmer's Palette–the first work of Egyptian art c. 2900 BC–in which the pharaoh is depicted as a giant in relation to all the other figures in the composition. In the present scenes, Kilgore is specifically framed in such a way as to make him dwarf everyone else around him, for he is meant to connote the same kind of iconic status as an American celebrity–those drive-in sized human beings of the Cold War–who wages war in grand Las Vegas-style spectacle. To the American mentality–and this remains true down to the present day–war and theater are indistinguishable, and Coppola highlights this by inserting himself into the scene in the role of a director whose camera eye will transform the carnage that he is filming into a scaled down miniature beamed through television sets back home (hence the televisual aesthetic is the very *opposite* of the ancient aesthetic which gigantifies that which is regarded as more spiritually important, for television scales *down* the important and has the domestic effect of making it seem banal, like the equivalent of an artistic ready-made. The battle, when it is viewed at home on television, will take on neither more nor less importance than the commercials for laundry detergent and toothpaste that the footage will be sandwiched in between).

Kilgore even deals out the cards from a playing deck exactly as a Las Vegas dealer would do at a gaming table: to his way of thinking, war is a game and a spectacle that should be played exactly like a game. Each dead person is assigned their playing card at the table: but it is only Kilgore who lives because the House always wins.

And then he relaxes on the beach at the barbecue, beer in hand, exactly as though he were an American working Dad just come home from a long day's work. The war is thus overcoded with the semiotics of the American backyard barbecue: beer and steaks for everybody, while exhausted soldiers sing drunken songs in the background.

Vietnam was the first televisual war, the first war to be scaled down and miniaturized into the cozy domesticity of the living room, although the images of fleeing Asian girls running from smoking ruins and dead American soldiers in body bags had a disastrous effect on the fabric of American society and contributed to its destabilization in the late 1960s by fomenting social discontent.

Down to the present day, though, Americans wage war on other countries as grand theater, for the ubiquity of the camera eye–from satellites to street-lights–has transformed the planet into a global Colosseum: the WikiLeaks footage of the Blackhawk helicopter attack in Iraq on civilians mistaken for insurgents (a couple of whom were Reuters newsmen) shows the real-life video-game glee with which the gunner mowed down his human targets, begging for permission from his C.O. to keep shooting.[27] And now with the current rise and proliferation of drones, video games are used to train these pilots as the nearest analogue to the electronic war, for their practiced computer gaze and trigger-rapid finger activity are precisely what the military wants for its drone "pilots."[28]

Kilgore, then, is the Wayne Newton of Vietnam, at once conscious of his performance before a planetary stadium of watchers and simultaneously a first-rate showman who never fails to deliver the goods. The gaze of the camera eye and the journalistic shutter enlarge him, just as they did for Elvis Presley and Marilyn Monroe, to the status of a planetary giant, a modern electronic Colossus of Rhodes whose feet stride over continents.[29]

Kilgore II

In this scene, Kilgore's Air-Cav regiment launches from the ground at dawn to the bugle cries of reveille. There follows a hypnotic, morphine-trance ride through the orange and vanilla swirl clouds as the helicopters head, in symmetric formation, toward Charlie's Point. As Kilgore and Lance discuss their preferences for light vs. heavy surfboards, the regiment approaches the tiny quiet village nestled in the jungle at the edge of the shoreline. Kilgore informs Lance that they will be playing Wagner about a mile out from the village, since it "scares the hell out of the slopes." Then, with the piece from *Die Walkure*–from the opening of its third act–playing at maximum volume, the helicopters glide in over the foam of the beach and begin demolishing the village, reducing it to rubble with mortar rounds, rockets, M16s and eventually, napalm. Keep in mind that all of this done so that Kilgore and his buddies can go surfing.

The first point to note about this (*very* famous) sequence–its influence is immediately evident the next year in the snow battle that occurs, likewise, about a half hour into *The Empire Strikes Back* (1980)–is that it is war fought under a single mighty C.O. with maximum strategic organization: the choppers attack with all the discipline of a highly regimented Roman military machine–such machines were composed of *both* cavalry and infantry, whereas the helicopters combine their separate lines into one phalanx–but when they touch the ground, the air-cavalry are instantly transformed into ground-based infantry as they are dumped out of the dromosphere.

The yellow crest which the Air-Cav pilots wear on the backs of their helmets is composed of a black stripe across a sun-yellow field with a tiny horse's head in the upper right corner. So we are to imagine that the mobilization of modernity has transformed ancient horseback-riding legions into the flying horses of Wagner's opera, since the Valkyries in Norse mythology ride on flying horses and swoop down to the battlefields to pick up the souls of warriors who have been killed in battle. The attack is thus structurally homologous to the old, *very* old story of Indo-European horsemen sweeping nomadologically across the ancient steppes of Central Europe and Asia, crashing into quiet farming villages everywhere they went, undoubtedly raping, burning and looting in the process, as we know that the Vikings did.[30]

The helicopter is, of course, much faster than the horse, but it still treats the space that it sweeps across in the same manner as the nomads do, that is to say, as "smooth space" (a la D&G's "nomadology" in *A Thousand Plateaus*)[31] and the villages and cities that are encountered in its path as "striated spaces" that interrupt their trajectories.

Willard and his crew—on the other hand—with their tiny gunboat that miniaturizes the *Argo*, are an anachronism from the days of the *Odyssey*, for they are sailors on a mysterious errand travelling through the snake-like arteries that lead through the back alleys, as it were, of the jungle; whereas Kilgore and his men are nomads of the skies capable of traversing any terrain whatsoever. The sailing vessel, like the man-horse-nomad assemblage, treats the sea as "smooth space," but the river is another matter topologically considered, for it is full of all kinds of striations, wadis, deltas and shallow spots where mounds of mud protrude. Let us not forget: the river is brown, whereas the sea is blue-green. The river is, therefore, a mixture of earth and water, and so its passage must be navigated with much greater circumspection than the great, glittering seas over which the Vikings prowled on their various raids.

Once his helicopter has touched the earth, Kilgore's ontological status transforms him from that of a Parthian (or Scythian, let's say) horseman to that of an enormous giant, as he strides across the beach and through the murky yellow and crimson-colored smoke of the battlefield. He shouts orders to his men to prepare the waves for surfing, but Lance insists that they should wait for the tide to come in. Kilgore replies that it would take six hours for the tide to come in, so he has his men drop explosives from their helicopters in order to simulate artificial waves like the surfing and beach theme parks in the American Southwest that generate mechanical waves with their machinery.

Kilgore calls in an airstrike to bomb the tree line, the very same tree line, be it noted, with which the film had begun, only in that case, the viewpoint was at ground level relative to the observer. In these scenes, the F-100 jets drop huge loads of napalm and transform the tree line into a living hell of burning fossil fuels and gasoline-perfumed explosives.

As Kilgore hunkers down and discourses on the virtues of napalm, a distant line of prisoners who have been scaled down by the camera's focus to tiny figures can be glimpsed marching across the beach behind him. With this image, Kilgore becomes a figure straight out of ancient myth and history, for the scene is a celluloid equivalent of the various military "victory steles" that have been erected throughout history, especially Mesopotamian history. The image reminds me in particular of the so-called Naram-Sin stele dating from the city of Akkad to about 2200 BC. Naram-Sin was the grandson of Sargon of Akkad, the founder of the Akkadian dynasty, and on the stele—carved out of pink limestone—Naram-Sin has the hubris to depict himself wearing the headdress of a god—with two bull's horns poking up out of it–while marching up the side of a mountain towards a pair of celestial disks that represent the domain of the heavenly deities. Enemies–a mountain people known as the Lullubi–are shown falling out of his way as he simply tosses them aside on his way up the mountain. Like Kilgore, Naram-Sin is the largest figure in the composition, for he is depicted–again with almighty hubris–in the semiotic slot that would normally be reserved in Mesopotamian art for deities, since they were always the largest figures in previous Sumerian compositions. Naram-Sin himself reigned for 36 years from 2254 - 2218 BC, and was the last great king of the Akkadian Dynasty before it was overrun by Gutian barbarians shortly thereafter. A whole literature surrounding the motif of "the hubris of Naram-Sin" later emerged, in which the subsequent collapse and fall of the Akkadian Dynasty was ascribed to his insolence toward the gods.

Naram Sim stele ~2230BCE

Kilgore is a modern incarnation of Naram-Sin: his manner of carrying himself and his command over his soldiers and equipment indicate that absolutely *no* signifier can escape the sweeping surveillance of his gaze. He is a human Panopticon, in full control of his battlefield, and *all* signifiers are held firmly in his grasp.

It is important to note that his tactical manner of fighting is to create and maximize a sort of maximal stress sphere over which, as the mightiest signifier in the zone, he has full command. However, as the film goes along, the entropy content of such zones increases with each sequence until it reaches full and total thermodynamic disequilibrium with the disorder of the Do Lung Bridge sequence. Each set piece becomes messier, and more and more disordered as the narrative unfolds.

The original theatrical release of the film in 1979 ended with Kilgore's complete control over his battlefield at the end of his napalm speech, but in *Apocalypse Now Redux*, the scene continues with the theft of his favorite surfboard, indicating the first small beginnings of an entropic element in his command, and correspondingly in the narrative episodes themselves. The board is stolen by Willard, who jumps with it into the gunboat, laughing, as he and the crew race away with Kilgore shouting after them. It is not so much the theft of the actual surfboard that angers him and sets him off in pursuit, but the fact that, perhaps for the first time ever, *a single signifier* has escaped his all-seeing capture and control, like a missing piece on an otherwise perfect chessboard.

The loss of the surfboard is thus the first entropic element to appear in the narrative, and since it is possibly the first time Kilgore the mythical giant has lost absolute control over a strategic and carefully managed battle zone, its implications are similar to the exquisite sensitivity to initial conditions in Chaos theory: a tiny crack in the quantum foam results in the asymmetric explosion of the universe. The theft of the board therefore suggests the appearance of a crack, not only in Kilgore's otherwise perfectly maintained command, but in the narrative episodes themselves, for each one, from this point onward, becomes more and more disordered as the story unfolds.

(0:52:09 - 1:00:35)
Mango / Tiger Interlude

In this scene, the crew are hiding in their boat under a grove of trees in a delta of the river while Kurtz flies overhead looking for them and demands the return of his surfboard. The sound of his voice through a megaphone disappears into the distance as the crew exchange banter, laughing about their hi-jinks. Chef has been fantasizing erotically about "mango cream pudding" in connection with Raquel Welch, so he decides to go off into the jungle to find a mango tree and Willard volunteers to go with him. While the two make their way across an almost alien landscape of gigantic, prehistoric-looking trees and heavy dark green foliage interspersed with fog, Chef tells Willard that he is in training to become a *saucier*, a cook who specializes in sauces. He is in the middle of a cooking school anecdote when Willard becomes suddenly alert and raises his M16, listening carefully and cutting Chef off in mid-sentence. Chef, frightened, whispers, "Charlie?" and the two wait nervously at the stirring foliage when a Bengal tiger suddenly leaps out of the bushes at them. The two flee back to their boat with Chef terrified and hysterical as the boat pulls away, Clean firing his gun randomly. The rest of the crew laugh when they learn that it was not "Charlie" who terrified Chef, but a tiger. "Never get out of the boat!" Chef yells, and Willard's voice-over narration comes on with deadly seriousness: "Never get out of the boat. Absolutely goddamn right. Unless you were prepared to go all the way."

The imagery of the film is now becoming more overtly primordial, bestial and zodiacal (whereas the Horse, only implicit in the Kilgore sequence, is the seventh sign of the Chinese zodiac, the Tiger–now explicit–is the third sign). Traditionally, in East Asian civilization, the tiger is an apotropaic image that is often associated with the gateways to temples and shrines–and also with tombs–for the tiger's ferocity scares away demons and those who are spiritually unworthy of entrance to the temple. Near the end of the film, when the crew pulls their boat into Kurtz's compound, we note the presence of two gray-colored stone tigers acting as threshold guardians at the top of the stone stairs. Chef is easily intimidated by the tiger, and it is perhaps no coincidence that he is beheaded by Kurtz near the end of the film (while Kurtz is wearing tiger-stripe makeup on his face), for his cowardice is neither spiritually admirable nor worthy of membership in Kurtz's court. Poor Chef gets eaten by the tiger after all.

The appearance of the tiger at this point in the narrative, however, signifies entrance into the Belly of the Beast, for the crew are actually *entering* into its mouth as they travel deeper into the jungle. In Taiwan, the Dragon and Tiger Pagodas that were built in 1976–at the same time as the film was being shot in the Philippines–feature two temples constructed out of seven storey pagodas erected side by side. To enter into them, one must step *into* either the open mouth of the dragon or that of the tiger, so that to enter the shrine is to enter the belly of the beast. The motif is also analogous to the scene in Steven Spielberg's *A.I.* when the passengers of the futuristic car race across the great bridge leading to Rouge City and enter through the wide open mouth of a giant female. (The city, as Lewis Mumford pointed out, is essentially female in that it is a container of human beings).[32] The difference, however, is that in *A.I.*, the protagonists were entering through the mouth of a goddess to gain access to a cosmopolitan environment where the instinctual-animalistic energies are normally repressed, but with the tiger scene in *Apocalypse Now*, the semiotics are the other way about, for the crew are descending into the deep realm of precisely such instincts and becomings-animal.

From henceforth, they will be travelling on the *inside* of the tiger, for the tiger is, in a way, the presiding spirit of the jungle and its ferocity.

As remarked earlier, the tiger in Chinese cosmology normally forms a binarity with the dragon: whereas the tiger is cosmologically associated with the West and with the element of metal, the dragon is associated with the East and with both wood and water. In a certain respect, then, the crew of the Navy PBR are riding on the dragon's back as they go upriver, but the jungle itself *is* the tiger.

And dragons, furthermore, are always in Chinese myth associated with water: there are four great Dragon Kings with palaces under the ocean, for instance, and the dragon which is cosmologically associated with the East, the blue-green dragon, is thought to sleep under the earth during the winter and when, in springtime, it emerges, it brings along with it the first of the spring rains. The rain that occurs at the end of the film after Willard has killed Kurtz may be regarded as the rain of the blue-green dragon emerging from the underworld to redeem the Waste Land with spring rains and renewal (whereas the White Tiger, in association with the West, brings death, like Kurtz himself vis a vis Chef).

If, however, one wished to consider the scene from a Freudian (rather than a Jungian) point of view, then we could say that the tiger would represent the punishing aspect sent by the Father (i.e. Kilgore) for the theft of his surfboard. There is a certain way in which the aggressive energy of the tiger reminds one of Kilgore, and in Chinese tradition, tigers are also associated with soldiers. So either reading is perfectly plausible.

Playboy Bunnies

This next sequence begins with Willard reading through the second dossier that he has received on Kurtz, while filling his water canteen with a bottle of Martinelli Cordon Bleu. He is offered marijuana by the crew, but he turns it down and closes himself off, preferring to drink, and think over the documents, alone. Willard resumes pondering the question of why Kurtz would join Airborne at "38 fucking years old," since the next youngest man in his class was half his age. If he joined the Green Berets, he would never get rank above colonel, but he did it anyway. And then he staged a major attack, called "Operation Archangel," which was paraded a major success by the media, and so forced the military to award him the rank of full Colonel anyway. Willard says that Kurtz received no special clearance: he simply thought the operation out and proceeded to execute it on his own. The operation is significant for showing the beginnings of Kurtz's autonomy from the military, and paradoxically, also the beginnings of his "fall" from grace with it, for they began to keep a close eye on him from that point on. Kurtz is the rebel angel whose azimuth of descent can be traced as precisely as that of Milton's Satan.

The crew then hear loud rock music as they round a bend in the river and an island of light surfaces into view before them: a central stage surrounded by floodlights, bleachers and large vulgar tubes of lipstick like Shiva lingams jutting up from behind the stadium.

The crew pull into the docks and approach the general store manager looking for some more fuel. He refuses to give them any unless they tell him their destination, but Willard insists that their destination is classified and shows him the papers from Com Sec and II Corps. The soldier ignores him, and suddenly Willard leaps at him–echoing the unexpected leap of the tiger from the previous sequence–and the man cools down very quickly, even giving him a bottle of whiskey to show "no hard feelings."

The show begins as a helicopter with the Playboy magazine icon printed on its nose cone descends onto a stage where a band is playing "Suzy Q" by Credence Clearwater Revival. The bleachers are packed with enthusiastic soldiers waving copies of pin ups of the girls from *Playboy* magazine, and on cue, a girl leans out from each side of the chopper: one dressed in a kitschy Native American outfit, and the other wearing a Cavalry shirt that echoes the uniforms worn by the soldiers in the Air-Cav sequence. After they jump out and begin dancing, a third girl is brought out by two soldiers who are holding M16s that she steps down from like Venus coming in from the sea on a half-shell. She is wearing a cowboy outfit and begins to mimic riding a horse as a sexual entendre. Again, the imagery of horse, cavalry, cowboy and the Native American who was decimated by the Americans with the same ruthlessness as the Vietcong play like thematic echoes in a Wagnerian opera as *leitmotifs* from the Air-Cav sequence, only now all the signifiers are recoded into an erotic context. There is even a white saddle on the nose cone of the Playboy helicopter. (Also, note that the rabbit is a lunar animal and in Chinese myth is directly associated with the moon: so, just as this sequence takes place at night with lunar / erotic symbolism, the Kilgore sequence took place in the daytime with solar / Martial symbolism like the yellow crest with the horse's head. And horses, too, have traditionally been associated with pulling chariots whose wheels were identified with the sun).

The crowd of young soldiers goes wild and soon shouts of "Take it off! Take it off!" can be heard, while Willard, with a bemused smile on his face sits down on the bleachers to enjoy the ensuing chaos. Two soldiers break past the barrier and jump on stage reaching for the girls, and they are followed by a flood of more soldiers, while the announcer cues for the helicopter to start up and herds the girls swiftly back inside the safety of the helicopter. The mob of young men follows as the helicopter rises from the platform, two of them clinging to one of its struts. Complete chaos ensues as men flood the stage fighting for access to the girls. (It is difficult to decide which motivating forces are stronger: those of Venus, in the present scene, or those of Mars in the Kilgore sequence).

The main point to note about the scene is that it represents an attempt to open up a Las Vegas-style "dome of spectacle" in the midst of a maximal stress war zone. In this respect it is the very opposite of what the Romans did with their Colosseums and hippodromes and gladiatorial arenas, which were attempts to open up maximal stress zones *within* the zone of cooperation represented by the city of Rome itself.[33] Here, it is the reverse: the Americans take entertainment and spectacle with them wherever they go, and so they are constantly attempting to re-verse small, local islands of war-entropy and transform them into the ordered lights and entertainment of vulgar theme-park style spectacles. Little has changed since the days of the Vietnam war as far as USO goes.

The scene can also be contrasted with the Kilgore sequence in a certain number of interesting ways: whereas Kilgore fought his battles as staged arenas with entertainment as supplements—surfing and playing Wagner wherever possible—the arena that is opened up in the clearing of the jungle by the Playboy bunny show is a highly ordered zone of pure entertainment that can only function by excreting war and maximal stress outside the system.

Once stressor factors–such as the mob of soldiers onstage–begin to enter into the system, it disintegrates.

Kilgore's battlefield, though apparently chaotic, was actually a highly organized zone of maximal stress over which he ruled as a Panoptic commander of all signifiers, a zone that was *so* fully under his control that he was able to intertwine it with American-style entertainment under the pretext that all surrounding maximal stress was neutralized by him. That sequence, however, as we saw, ended in *Apocalypse Now Redux* with the theft of Kilgore's surfboard and hence the beginnings of a motif of disorder in the form of an escaped signifier. In the Playboy bunny sequence, the scene begins with highly organized entertainment as spectacle that soon becomes disordered and ends in a state of maximum entropy and chaos as the soldiers storm the stage. In other words, the entropy content of each sequence begins to increase as the narrative unfolds into ever larger and larger fields of disorder and randomness.

When the soldiers shout for the three women to take off their clothing, they are of course merely erotically aroused. But the women do evoke the classical tradition of the Three Graces– Aglaia, Euphrosyne and Thalia–who were usually depicted naked and associated with rest, relaxation, play and amusement. R&R, in other words.

Raphael's painting of the *Three Graces*, from around 1500, shows all three graces nude and holding apples–possibly those stolen by Hercules from the Hesperides–although other art critics have associated them with the three handmaidens of Venus, the goddess of Eros, and the apples of discord that led the Greeks into the Trojan War.

So the Graces who, in Greek myth were associated with play, relaxation, rest and amusement, become the cause of erotic discord, just as the Greeks were led into the Trojan War to bring Helen of Troy back, since Venus had awarded her to Paris for

The Three Graces (Raphael ~1504)

judging her as the most beautiful of the three great goddesses, including Hera and Athene. The goddess Eris had tossed a golden apple inscribed with the words "to the fairest" during a feast of the gods at the wedding of Peleus and Thetis and Venus bribed Paris into awarding it to her, giving him the most beautiful woman in the world, Helen, in return.

The viewer has the sense, then, moving through the war with these two sequences—those of Kilgore and the Playboy bunnies—that it is a war firmly under American control, as organized and regimented as a Roman battlefield. The Americans simply export their civilization with them into the jungle, into the heart of its

Abgrund abysses, and conduct the war in those zones as extensions of their cosmopolitan way of life.

But as the boat moves upriver, this illusion will gradually disintegrate as the entropy content of each tableau increases, and the pockets and domes of civilization start falling apart and become less and less frequent as the disorder of the jungle slowly encroaches and supervenes on these microspheric zones of control and spectacle.

Third Dossier

In *Apocalypse Now Redux*, the following sequence, approximately ten minutes in length, differs remarkably from the 1979 version, for some things have been reedited and shifted around. The water-skiing of Lance, for one thing–with the Rolling Stones song "Satisfaction" playing on the soundtrack–had occurred much earlier in the film, but now it is placed after the Playboy bunny sequence, while Willard shuffles through the third dossier on Kurtz. He reads an important document that was written by Kurtz, entitled "Commitment and Counter-Insurgency (1965)," in which Kurtz articulates his philosophy of the war: "As long as our officers and troops perform tours of duty limited to one year," he writes, "they will remain dilettantes in war and tourists in Vietnam." And then the key phrase follows: "As long as cold beer, hot food, rock and roll and all the other amenities remain the expected norm, our conduct of the war will gain only impotence. We need fewer men and better. If they were committed, this war could be won with a fourth of our present force."

In other words, the philosophy of Colonel Kurtz differs from that of Lt. Col. Kilgore by 180 degrees. Kilgore's conduct of the war, as we have seen, consisted precisely in supplying his men with all the amenities: cold beer, rock and roll and hot food. Kilgore's attitude may be considered an extension of that of the US Army generally speaking, whereas Kurtz's life and mission, as the documents have been revealing to us, portray him as a serious and committed man with an almost monk-like attitude of piety toward the life of a soldier. If Kilgore was all about waging war as spectacle and entertainment, Kurtz's attitude is that of the spiritual warrior, stripped free of amenities and pleasures, and devoted wholly and purely to the conduct of war in an almost jihadist fashion. This is one of the main reasons for his attainment of autonomy from the military and its overcodings. As far as Kurtz is concerned, war should never be regarded as entertainment, but rather taken on with all the seriousness of a religion. He approaches it with a deadly earnestness that attracts to him a group of followers who are themselves "committed" to following his monkish and disciplined way of life.

In the original theatrical release, the next scene, in which a boat passes by Willard's PBR while a man's trousers fall and moon them occurred immediately in the wake of the Playboy bunny sequence when all the other PBRs were departing from the wrecked stage show. "Is that you, Lazzaro?" Chief shouts through his megaphone, while another boat glides past, tossing a smoke grenade onto their roof, which sets it aflame while Chef grabs a fire extinguisher to put it out (recall that his element is earth, which puts out fire).

During the following scene, while Clean plays a set of drumsticks on the metal wall of the pilot-house, Lance carefully reconstructs the burnt roof of the boat using dried palm fronds. This is significant because it represents the beginnings of the overcoding of the boat by the jungle. From this point onwards, the jungle begins to impose *its* own codes on the little boat and its crewmembers, who slowly begin to devolve under its influence, losing their civilized veneer and experiencing in slow motion the same transformation which Kurtz went through when he disappeared into the jungles and began to submit to the codes of its sign regime in place of those of the military.

The military and the jungle have two totally opposed sign regimes: that of the military is built up on a plane of axial organization with a hierarchy of rank, as we have seen. But the jungle's codes are those of the rhizome that undercuts and subverts all arborescent regimes with an *a*-centric carpet of horizontal forces that create a web of multiple power centers.[34] The jungle's sign regime, moreover, is invisible (despite the profusion of its strangling vegetation), and its nodes as centers of power can therefore irrupt anywhere, just as the tiger had done in an earlier sequence. The jungle, also like a rhizome, cannot be fought, since any part that is destroyed simply repairs itself and carries on, like an ant hive. The military's attempts to erect axial power structures–such as the Do Lung Bridge–are constantly undermined and subverted by subterranean and hidden forces which cause such structures to topple and fall. The jungle tolerates no center-periphery power structures, for its nodes are evenly distributed across the meshwork of its vegetation like a carpet. It welcomed Kurtz because he destratified himself from the arborescent hierarchy of military command and became a wandering node of power unto himself, a nomad drifting and flitting through the jungle like a wraith.

The overcoding of the PBR crew by the jungle, then, begins with this scene in which the apparently innocuous canvas roof of the boat must be replaced with dried palm fronds–i.e. substituted with jungle signifiers. Soon, Lance will begin removing his clothing bit by bit and painting his face like an aboriginal tribesman. And whereas Clean will be killed with a rocket, the Chief himself will be killed with a spear, one of the world's oldest and most archaic weapons, a weapon perfectly at home in the jungle.

The jungle, then, causes the veneer of civilization–which is much younger than the huge primeval forests with their gigantic overgrown trees and monstrous choking vegetation–to stiffen up like the shell of a cicada, and then to turn brittle and crack away, leaving a pulsing, glowing creature of pure aggressivity and violent primordial energies in its place. Kurtz was transformed into such a creature, and shed the brittle exoskeleton of his persona as a Green Beret colonel for the various becomings-animal of his new life as an emissary of the jungle's instinctive energies: a were-tiger, a bull, a dragon, etc.[35] Like a Mesoamerican shaman who can transform himself into a jaguar or an eagle at will, Kurtz has at his command a whole bestiary of animals that he can transform into, depending on what circumstance calls forth which animal: for instance, a tiger when he beheads Chef, a bull when he is sacrificed by Willard, or a dragon when he brings the rains at the film's conclusion.

The scene then returns to Willard going back through Kurtz's dossier, in which he learns that in the summer and fall of 1968, Kurtz's compound kept coming under attack by hostile Vietcong and was beginning to fall apart. That November, Kurtz then ordered the assassinations of four South Vietnamese commanders: three men and one woman. Enemy activity in his sector subsequently dropped off to zero. Note the occurrence here of another mandala: precisely *four* assassinations with the classic Jungian 3 to 1 formula, in this case, three men and one woman. (Whereas three of the PBR's four crewmembers will die; only Lance will survive from the boat's original crew).

According to the documents which Willard then continues to read, the army tried one last time to reign Kurtz in, but he had already broken off into the jungles to attain full and complete autonomy as a center of power unto himself (but actually as a node within the jungle's own network of riotous vegetal and animal powers). The army only ever heard rumors of him from captured VC, who knew his name by now and were terrified of him. In other words, he had, by that point, lost his substantiality in the three dimensional world of physics and devolved to become that of a shadow or an Egyptian *ka*, capable of becomings-animal at will. Later on in the film, we will see how Kurtz appears and disappears out of the jungle shadows unpredictably, for he is no longer an actual physical soldier but a mythic icon, or phantasmatic image, precisely the kind of image which Lacanian theory is erected–like the structures of the military–to destroy and eradicate from the psyche.

There then follows a conversation between Willard and the Chief in which Willard confides to him that though their actual destination is classified, the Chief will be taking him about 75 klicks upriver above the Do Lung Bridge, well into Cambodia, which is forbidden territory. Willard assures the Chief that he will then cut him and the crew loose, for he intends to set off into the jungles on his own to find Kurtz.

Medevac

Willard now reads a letter that Kurtz wrote to his son, in which he explains to him that the Army has officially accused him of murder (the assassinations of the four South Vietnamese officials). Kurtz points out the "timid lying morality" of the Army, knowing full well that it has only accused him of the assassinations because he didn't get any official clearance to do them. As the boat travels moodily upriver, going ever deeper and deeper beyond civilized zones, flakes and chips of entropic debris start to appear along the riverbanks: a local Vietnamese mother and her son drifting, ghostlike, in a Sampan, the son wearing the Air-Cav helmet that he has retrieved from the wreckage of a downed Huey, the charred and blackened skeleton of which still burns with incandescent flames in the trees above. Two or three of its crew dangle from the branches like bizarre upside down crucifixions, the riverbanks below them strewn with the detritus of the wreck, plastic wrapping, fuel cans, suitcases, food rations etc. etc. The Chief picks up the radio and starts trying to contact the local Medevac unit to notify them of the downed Huey and its KIAs.

As the boat drifts past, the carcass of the Huey burning in the trees evokes a similar scene from Werner Herzog's *Aguirre: the Wrath of God* in which Aguirre sees a Spanish galleon resting incongruously amongst the branches of a South American jungle tree as his raft floats past.[36] Thus, Coppola consciously folds *Aguirre* into his narrative as one text among many, along with *Heart of Darkness*, the *Odyssey*, *The Waste Land* and other works.

These texts function as Derridean marks of iteration which fold one inside the other like complex works of Japanese origami, pulled free and displaced from their original contexts to serve new functions in his own complex narrative. Thus, the "iteration" or "mark" of the Spanish galleon from *Aguirre* is removed from its narrative and transplanted to Coppola's film while undergoing transformation from a galleon to a downed Huey. Both narratives concern river journeys which end in madness, and the downed Huey is meant as a road sign pointing to the similarity of the outcomes in both narratives.

For Gadamer, remember, in his *Truth and Method*, the text is something that actually *loses* being with time, since there is no text-in-itself that can be understood objectively precisely because each age reads and understands the text in accordance with the parameters of its own zeitgeist.[37] There is no such thing as an "objective" reading of *Oedipus Rex*, for instance, since its semiotics change with the transformations of each epoch's different understanding of Being, of what it means for an entity, text, etc. to unconceal itself in the Clearing of its respective age. We can therefore never be certain that we have understood any text the way it was originally intended to be understood. It has vanished, for Gadamer, into a cloud of probabilities like a quantum wave function.

For Derrida, however–as I pointed out in the Introduction– the text *is* the universe, since the transcendental signifieds that once existed to anchor meaning for each age–the logocentric age, let's say–have disintegrated and thereby allowed the play of signification which Derrida termed "differance" to take place.[38] In that case, meaning is no longer localized to this or that specific epoch, for meaning now becomes potentially "infinite" with the play of escaped signifiers and textual citations. When an utterance or a mark is removed from another text, it creates a totally different text with new meanings, meanings that can never be exhausted due to the slippage of differance. The text doesn't *lose* Being, then, for Derrida, but *gains* it, since each text is holonomically composed of an infinite number of utterances from other texts, each one "folded" inside the other. The text, and not the cultural zeitgeist, is all there *is* for Derrida.

So it is not a process of each age understanding the same text differently for Derrida, because each age creates totally *new* texts from the ground up precisely by "folding" marks of iterability from all the others inside of it. Hence, *Apocalypse Now* is a celluloid matrix inside which all river journeys and sea journeys have been compacted and folded together to create a unique celluloid spectacle that is packed with an inexhaustible reservoir of meaning. No interpretation, not even my own, can therefore be fixed, final or authoritative.

The scene in the 2001 version—which, by Derrida's rules, is a completely different text from the 1979 version—now melts into the so-called "Medevac sequence" that didn't make it into the 1979 version because a summer typhoon swept through the Philippines and destroyed all the movie's sets. The blue-green dragon of the East from Chinese mythology, it seems, had come up from the underworld to pour its life-giving rains forth, with the exception that in the Medevac sequence it has "drowned" the M.A.S.H. unit-like set and transformed it into a work of complete desolation. It is the film's first true "waste land" image—ironically enough, since it is created by *too much*, rather than too little rain—and for the first time, we encounter a scene that *begins* in an advanced state of entropy. The rain-soaked tents are barely standing, propped up by sodden wood poles, and surrounded by stacks of hastily configured sandbag walls; the *disjecta membra* of civilization meanwhile—television sets, motorcycles, oil drums and so forth—have been washed downhill to the edges of the riverbank by muddy floods from the broken-up top soils near the tree line.

The helicopter with the Playboy bunny logo on the nose cone sits, looking dejected, on its landing pad, while Willard climbs out of the boat and is approached by two men covering themselves with plastic sheeting. Willard asks about their commanding officer, but they tell him that he was recently killed by stepping on a land mine and then they wander off, leaving a puzzled Willard in their wake.

Willard stands a moment looking around at the ruins of the Medevac unit and is just about to go back to the boat when the impresario from the Playboy show sequence opens a tent flap and invites him inside, saying there are some people he would like Willard to meet. Meanwhile, Lance, Clean and Chef wrestle with each other like boys amongst the junkheap, until Willard returns from the tent with a bottle of whiskey in one hand and a smile on his face. He tells them that he has just made a deal for the crew to trade two barrels of diesel fuel for the men to have a couple of hours with the bunnies.

Inside the bunny helicopter, Chef discovers his favorite pin up girl, Miss May–although he keeps referring to her as Miss December–who, to his disappointment does not have black hair but had been wearing a wig for the photo shoot. Strangely enough, she is surrounded by a collection of birds, and as he tries to position her to resemble the icon of her pin up, her breasts dangle seductively, resembling her original pin-up. When he kisses her, she lights up enthusiastically, claiming that he "kisses like a bird," and so he flaps his arms like wings as they begin to have sex. Meanwhile, Clean keeps tapping impatiently on the window outside the chopper for his turn.

In this scene, Chef, who is associated with the serpent via his cobra tattoo, achieves union with a bird-girl and in doing so, becomes, like Qetzalcoatl, the winged serpent. This marks him for certain death, though, since the serpent is a lunar animal that sheds its skin, just as Clean sheds his head when Kurtz, in *his* becoming-animal as a tiger, cuts it off near the film's conclusion. The characters, in other words, are beginning to devolve into their theriomorphic modes, as the animal vitality of the jungle slowly seeps its way inside them and brings forth their zoological equivalents.

Lance, meanwhile, has taken up inside one of the Medevac tents with another of the bunnies—the third is mysteriously absent and never accounted for—and it is in this scene for the first time that he begins to dabble with makeup, painting the girl's forehead while she lies casually on a bed complaining about things the sex industry made her do that she didn't like. Lance seems unconcerned and is having more fun with the makeup, which he now begins to apply to his own face. But when Clean taps with his rifle on the window, the startled girl jumps up and runs across the muddy floor of the tent, knocking over a casket from out of which spills the fish-belly-white body of a corpse. She takes refuge in Lance's arms, but Clean scares her again when his face appears in the window and when she asks, "Who is that?" he tells her, "I'm next, ma'am."

But apparently, his assignation didn't happen because in the next scene, when they are back on the boat, Chef is teasing him, saying, "I didn't know you were a cherry!" He insists that if he'd known Clean was a virgin, he would've taken him to a bordello in New Orleans, but Clean is angry for being skipped over, and the Chief has to intervene in their argument.

The Medevac sequence thus functions as an entropic contrast to the highly ordered and organized Playboy bunny show sequence that only gradually, near its conclusion, spiraled down into chaos. In the present scene, the three bunnies—one of which is missing—are trapped inside entropic conditions and are trying to exist in a camp that has been totally wrecked by the dragon's summer rains.

This is the first outpost of civilization that occurs in the narrative so far in which the jungle has already dismantled all the civilizational signifiers. The further upriver the crew go, the less civilization stands a chance against the almighty elemental powers of the jungle, which, one by one, dismantles and destroys all attempts to erect civilized outposts of any kind.

Note, too, that whereas the fire of the downed Huey in the trees ignited the Chief's concern–he corresponds to fire, as we have said–Lance, whose element is water, simply "surfs" his way through the chaos and wreckage of the Medevac scene with sheer insouciance. And he even comes away with the gift of the girl's makeup kit, which he then begins to apply–sitting at the boat's forward end–to his face in the manner of an aboriginal from henceforth. His devolution from the heights of American civilization to the depths of life in the jungle is in full swing, as the jungle and its combined tiger / dragon forces start to slip, slide and stir out from underneath them.

It is only Willard who is beginning to realize the almightiness of the elemental forces of the jungle which his mission has pitted them against, with its potential to strand civilization in its quagmire and to suck the psyche back down into earlier, more devolved forms of animalistic consciousness. He keeps away from the bunnies–wisely enough–but Lance and Chef undergo regressions, respectively, to becoming-animal and becoming-tribal as a direct result of their encounter with the girls.

(1:34:10 - 1:39:17)
Sampan

The gravitational pull of the jungle now sucks the crew downward over an event horizon of violence which implicates all five of them in a massacre.

"Sampan off the port bow!" the Chief announces: "Sampan off the port bow!" and when Willard questions him, the Chief tells him that local boats run supplies and guns through the delta and that it is the job of the PBR ("Patrol Boat River") to search and seize such shipments. Willard claims that his mission has priority here and that they wouldn't even be in this part of the river without his orders, but the Chief tells him that until they reach Willard's destination, he is just along for the ride.

When they pull alongside the sampan, it is apparently a simple farming vessel with three men and a young woman (once again, note the Jungian 3:1 mandala): it is loaded with ducks, a goat, chickens, and cans of rice and other vegetables. It is, in other words, a mobile farming village.

The Chief orders Chef to get on the boat and search it, but he stands on the bow pointing out the obvious: "There ain't nothin' on it, Chief." Rice, ducks, chicken, bananas, etc. But the Chief yells at him to get on the boat and conduct a thorough search, so Chef jumps onto it and starts throwing things around to prove his point: a basket of mangoes, a can of rice, a crate of dried fish. But the young woman is sitting protectively on top of a rusty tin can which the Chief thinks is suspicious, so he tells Chef to look in the tin can. Chef then shoves the girl out of the way but when

83

she runs back toward the can—and here, the crew possibly recalls the hat with the grenade in it that the young Vietnamese woman tossed inside one of Kilgore's grounded helicopters as it was picking up their wounded—Clean, alarmed by her sudden movement, starts firing the M60 machine gun, which sets off Lance, who, for a moment, has trouble loading his clip and then starts firing his M16 randomly until all three men are dead and the girl is wounded. Chef opens the tin can and pulls out a cream-colored puppy and says, "Look what she was runnin' for," while Lance reaches across and grabs the dog from Chef's hands. Chef is distraught and crying, but the Chief tells him that the girl is still alive and is moving behind him. He intends to take her to an ARVN to save her life, but Willard casually walks along the bow with a handgun and asks the Chief what he's talking about. "She's wounded," the Chief says, "we're takin' her to some friendlies, Captain." But Willard calmly tells Chef to get out of the way and fires a bullet into the girl, finishing her off, to the shock of the crew. He strides calmly back to the other side of the boat telling the Chief that he had told him not to stop here in the first place. "Now let's go," he says, and sits down on the starboard bow, with the setting sun burning a hole into the sky behind him. The scene fades out.

The Sampan sequence is a sort of miniaturized version of Kilgore's attack on Charlie's Point: the boat is itself a floating village, and although the crew's intentions are not hostile to begin with, they are pulled—almost entirely against their will—into a situation that replicates the decimation of the village by Kilgore. Whereas that battle had been conducted on the stage of the Big Other—collective, overwhelming, a clash of civilizations—the Sampan massacre is small, intimate and very much more painful. Kilgore, at the controls of the Big Machine of Western civilization, had reduced the crew of the PBR to mere spectators in a global Colosseum of state-sponsored violence and war played as a gigantic game of theater, but with the Sampan massacre, which is its miniaturized counterpart, each of the crewmembers is sucked into an act of collective violence that is more like one tribe against another. The violence is, therefore, very much more brutal and devastating to the crewmembers. Unlike Kilgore's planned attack-as-entertainment, the Sampan massacre *is* a legitimate "accident," but nonetheless it has the effect of transforming all the crewmembers into murderers. They are *all* now stained with primordial bloodguilt and none of them can claim innocence any longer.

Karmically speaking, *anything* can now happen to them as a result of being stained with primal bloodguilt. (Clean, on the M60, was the first to start shooting, and indeed, he will be the first to die in the film's second half).

This is the effect of the jungle, then, working its way into them, pulling them down into a sucking vortex, in which the brain's frontal lobes are dismantled, disrupted and pulled apart, while the fight or flight reptilian brain surfaces from out of its dark jungle *Abgrund* and begins to take control. The serpent leads point–though reluctantly–which is why it is Chef who must conduct the search, since his *vahana* is the cobra, an animal that is utterly at odds with his daylight persona of cowardice.

When Willard puts the final bullet into the Vietnamese girl's body, it is undoubtedly a mercy killing, since she would most likely have bled to death long before they had gotten her to the nearest ARVN. Nonetheless, it is cold, calculated and stunning to the crew in its casualness.

It is the snake upon which they are riding, coming to the fore. The further they travel up the Nung River, the larger loom the various becomings-animal of their natures, and correspondingly, the more morally depraved their actions become.

With the Sampan sequence, the Animal, with its zoological power struggles which know nothing of reason, civilization or compassion, is beginning to take control. The jungle is now inaugurating the process of undoing their civilized codes and recoding them with its own laws, while it dismantles the laws of the civilization of mechanized rationality that they are carrying with them. Those codes are cracking, stiffening up and beginning to fall away like the flakes of a stiffened exoskeleton, revealing the pure Animality that lies below the surface of such codes. *That* is the heart of darkness which too much time in the jungle brings forth. As a species, we came out of the jungles and spent four or five million years trying to erase its codes and replace them with the sign regimes of a civilized order. The cave paintings of Chauvet and Lascaux were the first attempts ever made–that we currently know of, anyway–to begin coding the Animal Within, surrounding it with signifiers like spears gathered around a doomed woolly mammoth.

But those codes are only thirty or forty thousand years old. The originary codes–the Adamic codes, let's say–evolved from the structural coupling of the body's genetic codes with those of the primordial jungles and forests of landscapes as devoid of civilization as Frederic Edwin Church's painting of the Cotapoxi volcanic landscape (1862), with its searing sun-hole and volcanic cone spewing ash across a dawn of man world horizon that is inconceivably ancient. *No* Heideggerian Clearings have opened up in such a landscape yet, only abyssal *Abgrunds*.

All that is required is enough time spent in the darkness of the jungle zones–even in the broad daylight of the Sampan scene–to reactivate those originary Adamic codes, which cause the coded flows of modern social formations to crack, crumble and collapse with seismic shock as the Adamic codes of the Animal rise to the surface once again, and overtake the personality with the sign regime of the jungle.

Kurtz is already all the way there, at the center of the jungle where no Clearing exists within which signifiers can unconceal themselves, but only an *Abgrund* abyss of primordial darkness and chaos over which he reigns as Lord.

As the crew of the little PBR travel towards him, they are being recoded into the gravitational pull of the collapsed singularity which he represents. They are *already* becoming followers of Kurtz without even knowing they're being inducted into his army.

Cotopaxi (Frederic Edwin Church 1862)

SECOND HALF:
THE JOURNEY TO
THE WORLD BELOW

The Do Lung Bridge · Clean's Death · The French Plantation Sequence ·
The Chief's Death · Arrival at Kurtz's Compound · The First Meeting with
Kurtz · Willard's Imprisonment · Chef's Death · Willard's Release From
His Imprisonment · The Hollow Men · The Sacrifice

The Do Lung Bridge

There was a point during the making of the film where Coppola was thinking of dividing his movie neatly into two halves, with the first half ending at the Sampan episode, to be followed by an old-fashioned theater lobby Intermission, and then the second half would resume with the Do Lung Bridge sequence. With that idea in mind, then, that is exactly how I have designed the present commentary, since at this point, we have arrived almost exactly halfway through *Apocalypse Now Redux*.

When the film fades back on, it shows a line of brooding black palm trees etched against a pale orange evening sky, with the boat headed morosely upriver while Willard's voice-over narration tells us that he knew the boys on the boat would never look at him the same way again after witnessing his heartless shooting of the Vietnamese girl. But he says that he now knows a few things about Kurtz that weren't in the dossier.

In the distance ahead of them, a night shot erupts with incandescent intensity as the flames and flares of the Do Lung Bridge surface into view, which Willard tells us is the last army outpost along the Nung River. Beyond it, there lay only Kurtz. The bridge is in a state of perpetual combat, and as the PBR approaches it, the sounds of gunfire and explosions can be heard more and more distinctly. Stranded soldiers dragging suitcases trail into the oily water towards their boat, begging for the PBR to stop and let them hitch a ride. "You'll get what you deserve!" one of them shouts prophetically as the boat motors past. Lance tells Chef that he has just dropped a tub of acid, and they gaze, awed by the spectacle of Perpetual War splayed out across the night before them.

The bridge is illuminated with wires of Christmas tree lights while ghostly floating flares sail out across it like Japanese lanterns. Explosions send up geysers of water from beneath the bridge, and towers of flame leap up toward it, while the wires connecting the towers echo with ricochets from one end to the other. Men periodically fall from the bridge, as it is shelled by enemies hidden somewhere in the darkness of the trees near the banks.

"Is there a Captain Willard onboard?" an army officer yells, approaching them with a bag of mail for the boat and yet another dossier from Nha Trang for Willard. The officer tells them that they are in "the asshole of the world" as he retreats into the gloom and disappears amongst the shadowy figures lining the riverbanks.

Willard decides to get out to try and find some more fuel—to replace the two barrels he had traded for the time with the Playboy bunnies in the Medevac sequence—and the Chief tells someone to accompany him. Lance, taking his puppy along, volunteers and follows Willard across the blasted, echoing landscape. The wire of lights going across the bridge echoes with ricochets as flames leap up from exploding grenades down below. Willard and Lance are transformed into charcoal sketches, with the flickering, strobing searchlights orbiting about them.

They descend into the trenches near the bridge, where the sounds of a loud electric guitar playing lost, random riffs blares out from a tape cassette recorder. Willard asks a soldier where the commanding officer can be found and the man yells back that he can be found at a "concrete fuckin' bunker" called "Beverly Hills" that is "straight up the road!" Lance inadvertently steps on the face of a man who he thinks is dead, but the man chides him and says, "You thought *wrong*, dammit!" It is not so easy to discern the living from the dead in this place straight out of Dante's *Inferno*.

Willard then comes across two black men behind sandbags firing a machine gun out into the darkness, while the voices of enemy Vietnamese shout insults back at them through the night. Willard's face surfaces out of the blackness like a rising moon as he asks the men if they know who the C.O. is: "Ain't *you?*" the soldier replies, flustered.

The single lone voice of an enemy Vietnamese can be heard shouting at them from somewhere out of the night's abysses, and the black men decide to go fetch one of their best marksmen, a man named "Roach," to take care of the situation. Roach appears to be in a drugged trance as he loads a rocket grenade into its launcher.

"Hey GIs, fuck *you!*" the Vietnamese soldier shouts through the night at them.

Roach pauses meditatively for a moment, raises his weapon, and then seems to be sensing for his target, until just the *right* moment strikes him and he fires his rocket grenade, which explodes into the night. After the explosion, there is only silence.

"Mother *fucker*," Roach says in order to punctuate his precise marksmanship.

"Hey soldier," Willard asks, "do *you* know who's in command here?"

"Yeah," Roach says vaguely, then wanders off into the shadowy murk and chaos of the trenches.

Willard and Lance then return to the boat and Willard tells the Chief, "There's no fuckin' C.O. here," while climbing into the boat. He informs the Chief that he didn't find any diesel fuel, but did manage to grab some ammo.

The Chief explains to him that Charlie blows the bridge apart every night, while the American soldiers build it back up again the next day, just so the generals can say the road is open.

"Just get us out of here," Willard barks at him and when the Chief asks him, "Which way?" Willard replies ominously: "You know which way, Chief."

And so the little PBR travels past the Do Lung Bridge, and its crew watch as the exploding fireworks burst into glowing shrapnel all about it as it collapses beneath a hail of blasts into the river behind them. The reverberations of its collapse echo through the water as the crew stares back it, aghast. Meanwhile, they head off into the uncertain darknesses of the night, a night which stretches out into an infinite abyss before them.

Whereas the Sampan episode had been a miniaturization of the Kilgore sequence—and the Playboy bunny show a retranscription of its signifiers into an erotic / lunar context—the Do Lung Bridge sequence is the exact inverse opposite of the Kilgore episode. Kilgore was the Commanding Officer who conducted his battles with complete Panoptic control of *all* signifiers: *nothing* escaped his gaze, and all signifiers followed the lines, codes and flows that he laid out for them to travel upon like light rays along geodesics.

The Do Lung Bridge, on the other hand, *has* no commanding officer to guide its signifiers along molar pathways: the signifiers are in a state of total chaos and maximum entropy has supervened. They are tracing and flying in all directions randomly, and all lines of communication connecting individuals to each other have been ruptured.

Recall how in the helicopter attack on Charlie's Point, the radios that were used to connect communications between one helicopter and another created an invisible field of electromagnetics that wove Kilgore's army together and kept it in organized formation. In the Do Lung Bridge sequence, on the other hand, all signifiers have retreated into their private spaces and nobody can communicate with anybody else. In place of connecting electromagnetic lines, there exists only the random blare of an electric guitar playing from a tape recorder that blankets all attempts at communication with a field of noise that one has to shout above even to be heard.

The Do Lung Bridge is war conducted precisely *without* a Kilgore–who would organize it into war-as-entertainment at one end–but also *without* a Kurtz, who would organize it as a guerilla-armed jihad with surgical strikes that hit precise targets and then get out with minimal chaos at the other. The Do Lung Bridge is war at maximum entropy, with no guiding lines of force whatsoever, and exists in between the spectrum of battle represented by Kilgore and Kurtz at opposite poles.

Willard calls it the "last army outpost," but civilization here has come totally unglued, with signifiers exploding and ramifying in all directions simultaneously. It is even more chaotic than the entropy of the Medevac sequence, which at least–with its feminine codes–harbored shelters in the form of tents and a helicopter within which to provide the individual a shell of some sort to take up refuge in. On the Do Lung Bridge, as exemplified by Willard repeatedly yelling at the drug-induced Lance to take cover, one is completely exposed and ontologically open to attack from all directions. There *are* no shells to hide behind, no exoskeletons to build. One is truly "unhomed" from the world in Heideggerian fashion.[39] No metaphysical systems exist here to protect the individual from the all-surrounding Chaos of infinite violence. It is pure nihilism, simple and complete. Indeed, we are well on the way to the movie's second half, with its journey to Avernus.

The officer who had delivered the mail to the boat told them that they were in the "asshole of the world," and indeed, in Dante's cosmology, he situates his Hell at the very bottom of the round earth, on the *inside* of its core, and no other episode in Coppola's film reminds the viewer so much of Dante's conception of Hell as does the Do Lung Bridge sequence. Indeed, it *folds* the "utterance" of Dante's Hell into the narrative, just like a pleat in a fold of clothing, along with all the other texts and utterances that it has folded into it with so many pleats.[40]

As promised, the entropy content of the narrative has, with this opening scene of Coppola's second half of his magnum opus, been completely maximized.

But from this point onward, all vestiges of civilization will disappear as the jungle with its sign regime completely overcodes and replaces that of the military.

All vestiges, that is, save one: the French Plantation Scene, which we will arrive at shortly.

Clean's Death

In a scene that is now flooded with lavender sunlight, the crew read through the mail which they have received at the Do Lung Bridge. Lance opens up a can of purple smoke and a dense cloud of it surrounds the boat, through which it floats like a dream barge on sunbeams. Chef reads a letter from his wife Eva, who has doubts about continuing their relationship across thirteen thousand miles, while Willard reads a letter from Nha Trang that informs him that a previous soldier named Captain Richard Colby had, just a few months earlier, been sent on a mission that was identical to Willard's. But Colby became a follower of Kurtz, for the military intercepted a letter which he tried to send to his wife, telling her to forget everything and that he was never coming home. It is a veiled warning to Willard of how easy it is to become seduced by the jungle's sign regime and to unplug from the paternal authority represented by the military and become overcoded by the female semiotics of riotous vegetation and primal urges. It also underlines the fact that his mission is not quite the singularity he had been led to believe that it was: indeed, it is a repetition of a mission that was already tried once and failed. Willard's mission, then, is not unique, but a repetition compulsion on the part of the military to try and kill Kurtz one last time in a covert manner.

Clean, meanwhile, has received a tape cassette from his mother, which he now plays while the boat drifts through the pink haze of purple mixed with gold sunbeams, and dense green foliage, thick with impenetrable trees, glides past along the riverbanks beside them. At once, and from out of nowhere, crimson-flared rockets begin soaring out of the tree line and the crew jump to their guns: Lance on the forward .50 caliber machine guns, Clean on the M60, while the Chief hits the gas and tries to give the boat enough speed to escape the rockets which chip and dent parts of his boat. One of the rockets hits Clean directly in the belly and within just a few seconds the attack is over and deadly silence prevails. The Chief notices that Clean has been hit and shouts for the Captain to tend to him. Chef leans over Clean's body, crying, while the eerie music on the soundtrack entwines itself around the scene like acoustic foliage. The Chief then steps away from the pilot seat while Lance takes the controls, and grieves over Clean's body while the tape recording of his mother, who is preparing for his homecoming, plays tragically in the background.

Clean is thus the first of the crewmembers to die as the jungle's immune system activates all around them and begins now to turn hostile to them, like the figures in Christopher Nolan's *Inception* who target the unwanted dream avatar who draws too much attention to himself. There is a connection with Clean's death to the Sampan episode, wherein he had been the first to pull the trigger on the M60 that killed most of the Vietnamese farmers aboard the fishing boat, thus staining him with blood-guilt. Clean may not have lost his virginity during the Medevac sequence, but in the Sampan massacre, he most certainly lost his innocence of the shedding of blood. (Note, too, that the dog, which was acquired during that massacre, has mysteriously vanished as a puzzled Lance wanders on the forward bow yelling, "Where'd the dog go?")

The Sampan massacre has changed everything: prior to it, the crew were all spectators to the violence and carnage around them. But after it, the primal sin of blood hovers over them like the cloud of purple haze released by Lance, and there is a definite sense of an increase in hostility toward them from the jungle itself. A new feeling of paranoia begins to settle over the men, and it is by no means unwarranted.

The imagery along the passing riverbanks slowly turns more and more mysterious, primitive and murderous. A dense fog begins to close around the ship, as though sent by the gods to punish them.

With the death, therefore, of Clean–the youngest of the crew–a new sense of doom begins to settle over the boat and its crew, and from this point on, they become hyper-vigilant, carefully scanning the passing banks for any further signs of immunological hostility.

We are speaking metaphorically here, of course, but it is as though the jungle itself were a living organism that is fully prepared to strike back if one directs aggression toward it or its native inhabitants.

The French Plantation Sequence

A dense blue-gray fog has now surrounded the boat as it drifts beneath the downed skeleton of a fighter plane, looking like some ruin from a forgotten civilization. As a pocket of the fog clears out, Willard, sitting on the bow, sees something up ahead and grabs a pair of binoculars through which he views the derelict remains of some once functioning station. As the boat pulls in to the collapsed dock, Willard climbs out, armed with an M16, and scouts through the apparently abandoned ruins as wisps of yellow fog trail through the corrugated and rusty shell of the station. A distant voice, speaking in French, comes yelling at them through the fog, to which Chef replies, "*Nous sommes Americains!*" He tells the Chief that they are French and begins to lay his weapon down, but the Chief barks at him to pick it back up. As the fog clears, a handful of men surface out of it like phantoms from the underworld, and their leader, a man named Hubert de Marais, welcomes them. Willard tells him that they have lost one of their crewmembers, and Hubert says, "We French always pay respects to the dead of our allies."

There then follows an impromptu funeral for Clean, whose body is wrapped in green plastic sheeting and his tape cassette recorder placed on his torso (exactly where it was struck by the rocket). A visibly distraught Chief folds the American flag while slices of sunlight cut through the lingering fog and hands it to Willard, saying: "Captain, accept the flag of Tyrone Miller on behalf of a grateful nation." Clean is then committed to the earth (his element, we recall, had been ether, the quintessence, or "fifth element," which has the property of turning with perfect circular motion, but it is the earth, the heaviest of all five classical elements, which now claims him).

During the ceremony, Willard catches a glimpse of a woman with short blonde hair peering down at them from the balcony of the second storey of the French house. (She will correspond to Calypso, the goddess with whom Odysseus was married on an island for seven years).

There follows a long scene at the dinner table where Willard sits beside the patriarch, Hubert, along with the rest of his French family. Hubert introduces the blonde woman, who comes down the stairs, as Madame Sarrault, as she sits down to join them for dinner. When Willard asks Hubert why they don't just leave their plantation and go back to France, Hubert explains angrily that Willard does not understand the French officer mentality. The French, he says, lost in World War II, they lost at Dien Bien Phu and in Nigeria, and Hubert and his family, which has lived at this plantation for seventy years, will *never* leave. It belongs to them; it is their piece of earth, and they will never cede it to anyone. Hubert tells him the number of people they have had to repulse during attacks while staying there: 58 Viet Cong, 12 North Vietnamese, 11 South Vietnamese and 6 Americans, which Hubert claims might have been "mistakes."

There follows a long discussion of political issues, such as why the French lost at Dien Bien Phu in 1954, while Madame Sarrault smokes a cigar and indicates her boredom by exchanging significant glances with Willard. One by one, the family retires for the evening until Willard is left alone with the beautiful Madame Sarrault who apologizes for her family and offers him cognac, which he refuses. They retire to the verandah, with its view out over the dark green vegetation of the coffee-brown river, and Madame Sarrault, who has been widowed, asks him if he knows why you can never step into the same river twice. Willard replies to the old question of Heraclitus correctly: "Because it's always moving."

The two then go up to Madame Sarrault's bedroom, where Willard lies on the bed with her as she prepares a morphine pipe for him to smoke. She explains that she used to do this for her wounded husband, who had been shot near his heart, and who used to rage and cry, and she would palliate him by explaining to him that there were two people living inside him: one who kills and one who loves. Her husband would ponder philosophically whether he was an animal or a god, and she says that she used to tell him he was both. (Note that Willard smokes from the morphine pipe although he had refused the cognac she had offered to him earlier, and also refused marijuana when it was offered to him by his crewmembers). Madame Sarrault tells him that he, too, is two people: one who kills and one who loves. She offers him more morphine but he is pleasantly entranced and requires no more, so she gets up to put it away. Then she undoes the hem holding back the muslin curtain around the bed, undressing as she walks around it, undoing the curtain at each of the four corners, thus creating a little cavern made out of fabric. Willard reaches out to touch her breasts through the thin fabric, and the scene then fades back into the fog with the crew on the boat, as though the whole episode had been a dream in Willard's clouded mind.

As explained in the documentary *Hearts of Darkness*, the French Plantation Scene was originally cut from the 1979 release because Coppola became frustrated with it (he didn't like the lighting, he didn't get the actors he wanted, etc.), but it is an important sequence for understanding how Willard, as he moves up the Nung River, simultaneously drifts ever farther away from the paternal authority of the military and the Name of the Father and, with the morphine ritual, creates a kind of pact or "contract" with the Mother to drive the Father out of his symbolic order. Madame Sarrault is the Jungian anima figure who provides the necessary alliance with Willard to unplug him from the overcoding of the military and its paternal authority. He is reconstructing a lost imaginal universe that the military had driven out with its Lacanian symbolic axis connecting him to the Big Other. But now, in an alliance with his anima image, he is reconnected back to the imaginary axis that Lacan's theory is designed specifically to dismantle and destroy. Madame Sarrault is the muse of the jungle, a kind of disguised river goddess in alliance with whom Willard drives out the Father and begins to reconstruct an axial pathway to the inner world of dreams and myth. (This is why she asks him about the mystery of Heraclitus's flowing river, for she herself *is* the river in personified form. Indeed, most of the rivers in Asia are named after goddesses, just as Joyce refers to the River Liffey in *Finnegans Wake* as the flowing primordial energy of Time itself as a goddess).

Note that the structure of the scene replicates the opening scene of the film in which Willard lay in his bed, gun at his side, burning a hole with a cigarette through a picture of his ex-wife, and in a mode of complete self-destruction. In the present scene, Willard is back on the bed where he started, only now his wounds are being healed by the compact he makes with his anima to undo the codes that the military has placed upon him by blocking all access to the imaginary order.

Madame Sarrault does not come from the Symbolic Order, and she is not a hallucination from the Real. She *is* the Imaginary Order incarnate, the Jungian collective unconscious that spews forth myths, dreams and images which serve to guide and shape the individual's life, an entire world of images which Lacan does not trust and specifically "crosses" out with the "X" of his L-schema. Now Willard is recovering that very imaginal order, and his muse is healing the wounds that he inflicted upon himself in the film's opening. Whereas he had punched the mirror with his right hand, he now reaches out with his left hand to touch Madame Sarrault's life-giving breast, for the right hand belongs to the paternal order while the left belongs to the realm of the Mothers. (The Tantric path, in India, for instance, is known as "the Left Hand Path.")

Madame Sarrault, furthermore, forms a classic 3:1 ratio with the three Playboy bunnies who had appeared earlier in the film as sex objects. Madame Sarrault, by contrast, is no sex object and will not be treated like one, for she has the depths and soul which the bunnies did not have and she cannot be pushed around. She is the feminine equivalent to Willard and makes a perfect (though brief) companion for him in this miniaturization of the Calypso episode out of the *Odyssey*.

This episode, furthermore, is the one exception to the rule that as the crew journey upriver, each sequence becomes more and more entropic and less and less civilized. The French Plantation is a sort of dead museum out of the nineteenth century, frozen in time. There exists a kind of protective microsphere surrounding it and preserving it from entropy, so that it becomes a sort of pocket or bubble that is immune to the ravages of the entropy surrounding it. It is an ironic contrast to Madame Sarrault as the river goddess of Time, for the Plantation itself exists in a bubble *outside* of time. It has been set aside by the gods and preserved as a kind of magical island for rejuvenation.

Coppola, with his fog-machine effects, specifically gives the characters a ghostly, phantom-like quality, as though we were visiting yet another level of the Underworld. It is appropriate that the sequence begins with the burial of Clean here since that scene functions as a kind of entryway into the realm of Hades. So, though the entropy content has been momentarily reversed, we are still down in the Underworld here, for the entire second half of the film differs from the first half in having the quality of a *nekyia*, or Journey through the Land of the Dead.

Willard, now healed and rejuvenated by contact with the river goddess, can proceed on the rest of his journey up the river, having been given a sort of magical aide with which to enable him to confront Kurtz, just as Calypso gave to Odysseus wine and meat before his departure from her island. Through contact with the regenerative powers of the feminine, that is, he is recentered with a new alliance made with the sphere of Mother Right which will enable him to stand on his own in his confrontation with the rebel angel, Kurtz.

(2:19:48 - 2:25:20)
The Chief's Death

The dense blue-gray fog has resumed and Willard is sitting on the forward bow with the M16 in almost the exact position he had been in at the start of the French Plantation Sequence. The sounds now, however, can be heard of tribal chanting, singing and dancing from the immense darkness of the entangled tree line on either side of the river banks. A terrified Chef–he is *always* terrified–asks, "Why don't they just fuckin' attack, man?"

Werner Herzog pays homage to this scene–which comes straight out of Conrad's *Heart of Darkness*–when, in his 1982 film *Fitzcarraldo*, he has Fitzcarraldo travelling by steamship up the Pachitea River, a tributary of the Amazon. His crew, for the most part, have deserted the ship, being superstitious about the legendary Jivaro tribesmen. Fitzcarraldo and his Captain and the engineer are all that remain, and the sounds of tribal drums can be heard from either side of the riverbanks. Fitzcarraldo's response is an interesting one, though: he retrieves his gramophone and plays Caruso singing opera at full volume back at the trees, to which the response is a sudden silence. Eventually the tribesmen surround the steamship with their canoes and approach, hailing it as the vessel of the gods which their myths have prophesied.

In the present scene of *Apocalyse Now*, however, the fog clears to reveal a new landscape: for the sun-washed riverbanks are now lined with altars like totem poles stacked with bull's horns. They adorn the green hills of the sloping shoreline in dense profusion, and local Montagnard tribesmen, moreover, are now visible hopping and jumping in and out of the trees.

From out of the dead museum of the French Plantation–a relic from the nineteenth century–the crew have emerged into the world of tribal man, a world whose semiotics were explored systematically at the end of that century with the laying out of the ground rules for the discipline of anthropology. All civilized signifiers have receded beneath this wash of tribal imagery, which now overcodes them by what D&G term in their book *Anti-Oedipus*, "the primitive territorial regime,"[41] a sign regime which codes all flows on the full body of the earth itself. In an orally based society without writing, that is, the totem poles of the bull god function like graphemes that are inscribed upon the earth itself as a kind of writing that territorializes the very ground with the codes of the jungle and its gods.

Suddenly, arrows are shot at the boat from both banks, and the air is filled with the sounds of their whizzing. Lance hits the forward .50s and Chef his M16, but Willard realizes that they are not true arrows, but sticks and he tells the Chief that they are just throwing sticks to try and scare them and to order the men to stop shooting. But the Chief steps out of the pilot-house, evidently to pick up a weapon, while a figure can be dimly glimpsed on a hill of the riverbank behind him hurling a spear that punctures through the Chief's back and erupts through his chest with deadly violence. The Chief, taken by surprise, has only enough strength to whisper, "A spear," and then falls down to the deck while Willard holds him. The Chief, however, does not go easily: he reaches up and grabs Willard as though to try and drag Willard down with him into his death and so Willard is forced to defend himself by pushing the Chief's head back until his breathing stops.

In the next scene, the boat is temporarily beached while a cloud of purple smoke floats about it once again, so that Willard can climb down and begin his trek alone into the jungle. He is prepared to set off to find Kurtz by himself, after explaining the true nature of his mission to Chef. "I'm going into Cambodia," he says. "There's a Green Beret colonel there who's gone insane and I'm supposed to kill him."

Chef's reaction is typical: he throws a fit, yelling about how he thought Willard was going to do something important like blow up a bridge or some railroad tracks. Willard makes to leave, but Chef, terrified (once again), tells him that he and Lance will go up there with him, but *on* the boat. Nothing frightens him more than the prospect of the jungle and its horrors: "We'll go up there with you," he says, "but *on* the boat."

Lance, meanwhile, is busy giving the Chief a watery funeral. He hums a dirge and gently places the Chief's body into the se- rene limpid river water which mirrors the ghost of a liquid sun. Lance watches as the Chief's face disappears like a deathmask be- low the water. Lance, as we have said, corresponds to water, and the Chief to fire, and so the Chief's fire is put out by his burial in water. Whereas Clean's burial had been into that of the earth, the heaviest of the classical four elements, the Chief's is water, the next heaviest element after earth. Chef's death by beheading (air) will follow with the next heaviest element in the sequence, while fire, the lightest of all four, will be used when Kurtz's compound is bombed over the film's closing credits by an airstrike.

The entire sequence is a bit like a replay of the attack on the boat with rockets, but the difference now—and this scene is taken straight from *Heart of Darkness*—is that arrows are a much more primordial ballistic missile than rockets. They originated, perhaps, sometime during the Lower Paleolithic, while the spear may have been invented as far back as the time of the Neander- thals. Thus, the codes of higher civilization are slipping away: the spear that kills the Chief is the tactical counterpart of the bull god totems which are the graphemes inscribed onto the body of the earth in place of writing in an oral-tribal culture. Rockets have devolved into spears; dossiers into tribal altars-as-signifiers of Kurtz's domain.

The jungle's immune system has activated once again and now one more crewmember has been claimed as the boat drifts ever closer to the tribal kingdom of Kurtz, the god of these bull's horn altars. In Conrad's novel, *Heart of Darkness*, we are told that Kurtz ordered the arrow attack to try and stop Marlow (Willard's counterpart, which is almost, but not quite "Marlow" sounded phonetically backwards, i.e. "Wolarm") from coming to take him away, where he is similarly lord over a tribal kingdom, although not a military, but a mercantile ivory trading operation. In *Apocalypse Now*, it is likely that Kurtz has sent these tribesmen out to try and stop Willard's mission before he gets too close. As proof of this, the careful eye will catch the photojournalist played by Dennis Hopper jumping along the shoreline, snapping photographs.

But Kurtz's immune system, with its jungle-as-extension of his anatomy, is beginning to weaken, and he knows it. Willard is the virus that *will* get through the immunological defenses this time and Kurtz is preparing to meet him.

For his days are numbered.

Arrival at Kurtz's Compound

The remains of the crew now proceed up the river toward Kurtz's compound while Willard's voiceover narration tells us that he didn't know what he would do when he confronted Kurtz, but whatever it was it wouldn't be the way they'd called it at Nha Trang. He begins destroying the dossiers sent to him by II Corps as the boat floats spectrally up river and the banks become almost like yawning dark canyons to either side.

The boat rounds a bend into a clearing where Kurtz's compound finally surfaces into view. They are confronted at first with a swarm of natives standing in their canoes, natives whose bodies have all been painted white, the color of the dead ancestors. They are a collection of spectral figures and Willard warns Lance to keep away from the guns as the canoes separate to allow the PBR to float through.

The very air itself appears to be stained with vanilla coloring, as leafy palm trees lean this way and that above the stone steps leading up to the entrance of Kurtz's domain. He has occupied the ruins of an Angkor Wat-style Cambodian temple, with stone tigers as threshold guardians on either side of the steps. Dusty yellow smoke hovers in the distance to the left, and a soft pink smoke drifts beyond the palm trees to the right. A hanging body, with military shirt and no pants on dangles from the branches of one of the trees. Kurtz's disheveled Montagnard army awaits them on the steps: women, children, ex-soldiers, etc. Leafy huts with peaked roofs on towers made out of stilts rest beneath the gaping abysses of massive green trees with vertebral-like spines.

Chef, wearing a greenish-yellow leaf frond on his head, steers the boat into the dock as the photojournalist played by Dennis Hopper steps forth and warns him about mines to either side of the steps, and the monkeys that bite. When Chef says he isn't coming in there because they were attacked, Hopper tells them to "zap 'em with the siren," which Chef does, and the Montagnards stir and rustle a bit, but not much else as the boat drifts into the dock and Hopper jumps onboard.

"I'm an American!" he says proudly. He is based on the harlequin character of Conrad's novel whose clothing had been a patchwork of multi-colored fabrics. But Hopper's patchwork consists of three or four cameras that dangle from around his neck. He is wearing a red bandana and is on the lookout for cigarettes. He tells them he is a photojournalist who has been in Laos, Cambodia, Vietnam and has been covering the war for years. His patchwork, then, is a media collage of photographic images.

Chef accompanies Willard onto the stone steps, upon which someone has inscribed in white lettering the words "Apocalypse Now." Dead bodies are strewn about the lintels of the steps near the stone threshold guardians.

Hopper (whose character's name we are never told) tells Willard that "these are his" people and that they are afraid that Willard has come to take Kurtz away. Hopper rambles on in broken sentences about the almightiness of Kurtz and his brilliance. When Willard says that he just wants to talk to the colonel, Hopper points out that one doesn't talk to the colonel, one only listens.

Willard spots Captain Colby standing with a group of soldiers, women and children. They are surrounded by lush vegetation and lemon-colored smoke that floats lazily through the air.

"Colby," Willard says, as Colby stares back at him, wordlessly and in reply seems only to clutch at his rifle insecurely.

"He feels comfortable with his people," Hopper says, still discoursing upon the wonders of Kurtz. But then he notices that Willard has spotted severed heads littering the steps that lead up into Kurtz's temple. In the novel, *Heart of Darkness*, Marlow sees a row of heads on spikes through a pair of binoculars adorning the front of Kurtz's mud hut, but in the present film, the heads are scattered everywhere. "Sometimes he goes too far," Hopper says. "But he's always the first to admit it."

When Willard reiterates that he only wants to talk to Kurtz, Hopper says, "Well, man, he's gone away." Willard says they'll wait for him, and he tells Chef that they will return back to the boat for a while.

Like the Do Lung Bridge sequence, the viewer has the sense of a place that has gone totally awry, and exists in a state of maximum entropy, although no combat is taking place. Instead, there is an eerie, dreamlike silence that hovers over the giant trees and the chipped stone steps of the Cambodian temple. The entire compound is in fact a three-dimensional externalization of the contents of Kurtz's mind. It is a mind that has gone insane, with splinters of wild thoughts, irrational ideas and primal violence exploded across neurons like the remains of a battle zone. The compound itself, therefore, externalizes Kurtz's mind: signifiers have shot in every direction with no logic or rational purpose for why they have gone that way. Bodies hang from trees and heads are littered about as signifiers that have been removed from logical and natural contexts and crossed zig-zagging lines of flight that have collided into each other. It is a place that only a madman would preside over, a kind of center of the Underworld where the lord of the dead–Osiris, let's say, or Dante's idea of Satan stuck upside down in the earth's core–reigns.

It is truly an apocalypse in the sense that it is the end of the river, and apparently the source of all its lunacy, violence and irrationality. In arriving at Kurtz's compound, Willard has actually discovered the source of the insanity that is leaking from it and radiating against the current all the way out into Vietnam. Every moment of lunacy and visionary destruction, from Kilgore's antics to the chaos of the Do Lung Bridge, has its source *here* at Kurtz's compound, as though his mind were emanating its evil influences out across Vietnam and Cambodia for hundreds of miles. It is Kurtz who is the source of the insanity of the Vietnam War, a war which, somehow, has projected from his mind like the physical world that radiates from the mind of the dreaming god Vishnu, whose sleep is our waking reality. Indeed, there is even a stone statue of the god Brahma, the Indian god with four faces which sits on a lotus that emanates from the sleeping god Vishnu and sends the radiant energies of his dream beaming out with his four faces into the four directions of the world. The stone pillar shows only the face of a god, but we know it is Brahma because the face is represented on all four sides, and it is the symbolic source that radiates the lunatic energies of Kurtz's mind outward across the blasted landscapes and ruptured lines of the Vietnam War.

Here at last is the source of *all* the lunacy which they have encountered in episode after episode; the source of the increasing entropy that has randomized places like Do Lung or the Medevac unit; the madness that causes the massacres and bombings of the villages and sampans of the war. For Kurtz *is*—on the imaginal plane, anyway—a kind of god, the god at the heart of the *Abgrund* concealed in the darkest depths of the jungle beyond all the Great Walls which civilization has tried to *keep out*.

"And this also," Marlow begins his narrative in Conrad's *Heart of Darkness*, referring to England, "has been one of the dark places of the earth," for in Roman times, England was a land of savages and primordiality that existed beyond the *limes*, beyond the pale of civilized rationality that Rome in those days stood for. Whenever a general or a tax collector or a private adventurer was sent out into the dark forests of England, he knew that civilization would not be with him and that he would have to make his way through the chaos of the Gauls and the barbaric customs of the Celts; he would have to wade through forests of infinite darkness where no civilizational Clearings exist as spaces of encounter between entities on a philosophical plane a la Heidegger. Only darkness, human sacrifices, fog, distant gloomy camp fires and an impenetrable abyss which the light of Rome could never illumine.

Willard now finds himself in the role of Marlow's proverbial tax-collector, who has now found himself way, way beyond the pale of the civilized world. He has entered another kind of Clearing, a Clearing in which entities unconceal themselves only with nihilistic ferocity and for which and to which absolutely *anything* can happen. There is no escape, no home, no shelter, no protective macrosphere to guarantee one's safety.

Willard is realizing that he is in a place where morality does not exist, and where all decisions are made for the sake of lunacy. He has arrived, at long last, at the narrative's heart of darkness, an *Abgrund* abyss that is so deep and fathomless that he has now no idea what to do. He is not even sure whether to carry a weapon with him, since he knows it would avail him no purpose.

And Kurtz, who sits backs in the gloom of his temple, knows this.

And waits for him.

The First Meeting with Kurtz

Chef and Willard have now returned to the boat, where Lance sits on the forward bow clutching a spear and looking more than ever like an aboriginal. All military codings have been withdrawn from him, for the jungle has already taken him into its *Abgrund*. The key element for this scene, moreover, is water, and that is Lance's element as a surfer.

Chef volunteers to kill Kurtz for Willard, but Willard tells him to stay on the boat and to use the radio to call in an airstrike if he has not returned by 22:00:00 hours. Then Willard, cigarette dangling from his mouth while rain pours steadily across the soggy vegetation, attempts to approach Kurtz's compound, but he is surrounded by Kurtz's army, who are chanting ritualistically as they grab him and turn him upside down and drag him through the mud in a second baptism that undoes the military overcodings of the shower scene baptism at the start of the film. At this point, Willard has *exited* the US Army and is now free of its codes–he has already formed an alliance with the Mother in the French Plantation Sequence–although he is not yet aware of the implications, namely, that he is free to do anything he wants. He is no longer a mere appendage of the military, an organ that it uses to reach like a hand into the jungle to pluck Kurtz like a piece of fruit from one of its trees, for the baptism in mud frees him in a manner that is analogous to cutting an umbilical cord.

Nevertheless, he is taken prisoner by the Montagnards, who bind his arms behind his back as they take him into Kurtz's inner sanctum, a dark, shadowy room that seems to be composed of dingy yellow light mixed with black chiaroscuro. Willard is pushed to his knees and sits there in front of Kurtz, who reclines on his bed, surrounded by stone pillars. He is a huge, rotund figure garbed in black and his face is not at first visible, but as he sits up and the bed creaks with the shifting of his weight, all the viewer sees of him is the round bald monk-like head that looks as if it might have been carved from ivory.

Kurtz asks Willard where he was born, and Willard tells him that he was born in Toledo, Ohio. The sound of constantly running water can be heard in the long silences between their exchanges.

Kurtz then recounts a sort of mirror image of Willard's river journey by explaining how he himself once went down the Ohio River as a child in an area that was near a gardenia plantation. It looked to him as though heaven had fallen to earth in the form of gardenias.

Then Kurtz sits all the way up on the edge of his bed, though the viewer still cannot quite make out his facial features, and cups his hands into a bowl of water in his lap and begins—in a kind of mimicking of Willard's new baptism—to pour water over his smooth bald head as he asks Willard whether he has ever considered the possibility of any real freedoms, not just freedoms from the opinions of others but freedom even from the opinions of himself.

Willard remains silent, for he is unaware of his new ontological status as an Individual who has come unplugged from the paternal authority of the military.

Kurtz then asks him what reason the Army gave Willard to terminate his command, and Willard tells him that they said he had gone totally insane and that his methods were unsound.

"Are my methods unsound?" Kurtz asks.

"I don't...see any method at all, sir," Willard replies in a line taken from Conrad's novel.

Kurtz then tells Willard that he expected someone like him, but he wants to know what Willard expected. When Willard does not reply, Kurtz turns to look askance at him and asks him if he is an assassin.

"I'm a soldier," Willard replies.

"You're neither," Kurtz says, and for the first time his face emerges in half-shadow from the gloom. The viewer sees only half of Kurtz's face, with its one vacant staring eye, an eye that is weirdly unfocussed, as though it were seeing something inaccessible to physical vision, some inner phantom perhaps. It is an eye that very much looks like that of a madman. Kurtz tells Willard that he is merely an errand boy sent by grocery clerks to collect a bill.

The scene is structurally homologous with the Judgment of the Dead in the Egyptian Afterlife in which the *sahu*, or astral body of the dead person comes to the throne of Osiris for judgment and his heart is weighed on a scale against a feather. If the heart is heavier than the feather, the soul is devoured by a crocodile demon known as the Swallower. If the feather is heavier–that is to say, if the individual has lived a more spiritually motivated than physically motivated life–then Osiris pronounces judgment upon him and assigns him to a specific place in Amenti, the Egyptian underworld.

The constant theme of water in the scene–Willard's baptism, Kurtz's self-baptism, and the continual sound of running water–indicate that the scene takes place in the abyssal realm that lies *below* the physical world. In Mesopotamian cosmology, the entire earth was imagined to be a flat disc that rested on the infinitely deep waters of the *abzu* governed by the god named Ea, who was half-fish, half-man and later became the sign of Capricorn in the zodiac.

In the semiotic vacancy of the feather, however, the spiritually pure symbol of the white gardenia substitutes as the counterbalance on the scale of Kurtz's judgment of Willard. He tells him that he is merely an errand boy to reduce his ego to the status of a military servant, but it is designed to help free him from such servitude and to allow him to attain true independence by seeing how he has been used merely as a pawn on a larger chessboard. Kurtz is attempting to rupture the "significative closure" that Willard's life has arrived at ("The End," that is, from the film's beginning), and to introduce him to new anthropological types and imaginary significations that will open him up for rebirth.

(2:42:17 - 2:45:12)
Willard's Imprisonment

A man stands spewing the arc of a flamethrower randomly as Hopper comes walking along a road that has been constructed against the edge of a cliff and bordered by a line of sandbags. Along this Via Dolorosa–as it were–the corpses of crucified men, propped on bamboo slats nailed to palm trees line the path as Hopper walks with determined stride up the steep slope near Kurtz's temple. Amongst the crucifixions, an area has been set aside for prisoners who are locked into bamboo cages standing up (thus echoing T.S. Eliot's line in *The Waste Land* that reads "here one can neither stand, nor lie, nor sit"). Hopper goes directly to the cage that Willard has been imprisoned in and holds up a cup of water for him to drink, asking Willard why such a nice guy like him would want to kill a genius.

Willard says nothing in this scene, for it is entirely Hopper's monologue, but much of the imagery of the monologue has been taken from Conrad's novel.

"He's got something special in mind for you," Hopper tells Willard as he gives him a drag off of his cigarette. Willard looks wasted, depressed and more exhausted than ever before.

Hopper also tells him that he knows something about Kurtz that Willard doesn't know: though Kurtz is clear in his mind, it is his soul which has gone mad (another line from the book which the harlequin figure tells Marlow). He also explains to Willard that he thinks Kurtz is dying and that he hates "all this," referring to his compound and the Waste Land that he has gener-

121

ated as a result of his own insane actions. Hopper then tells him that Kurtz likes him, otherwise he would already be dead and he must therefore have something special planned for him.

"When he dies, it dies," Hopper tells him, gesturing out at the jungle, and apparently rambling. "Because what are they gonna say when he's gone? That he was a kind man? That he was a wise man? Bull*shit*, man!"

Hopper then points at Willard emphatically and says, "*You.*"

Willard in this scene, then, is in the role of the Gnostic myth of the soul that has been sent on a mission into the earthly world and ends up getting captured and fallen into matter, where it then forgets its original mission.[42] But the imprisonment is only temporary and it is designed as a gesture on the part of Kurtz to teach Willard that he has been in a prison all his life working as an assassin for the US Army.

He *does* have special plans for Willard, for he knows that Willard is going to kill him and he has already acquiesced in this. But he wants the assassination to be an act of *free will* chosen on Willard's part as the result of his coming unplugged from the paternal authority that he is no longer bound by. Like one of Michelangelo's captive slaves, Willard has been bound by Kurtz, but only so that he can arrive at the decision to kill Kurtz *on his own* and not as the result of an act on behalf of the military who has sent him to do the job. Kurtz knows that if Willard kills him, it will be as the result of a decision that Willard has arrived at on his own, using his own newfound free will and that he will therefore have to bear the moral consequences of the action for himself. It is not something that can be deferred to the responsibility of the military.

It will not be under the Name of the Father that Willard kills Kurtz, but in alliance with the Mother, that is to say, from out of the *Abgrund* or abyss of freedom—as Schelling termed it in his philosophy—that lies within each and every one of us as a zone for introducing new chains of causality into the otherwise mechanistic cause-effect chain normally governing the laws of matter. Only the human being, as far as both Kant and Schelling were concerned, has the true freedom of will to introduce Acts that function as Singularities in the Law-governed and deterministic realm of Nature. Willard has lived his life thus far like a billiard ball bouncing in reaction from one cause inflicted upon him by the military after another. *This* killing, his seventh–and last–will differ from the other six in that it will not be the result of mechanistic determinism, but a true Act of the Will in the highest philosophical sense.

That is what Kurtz wants Willard to realize.

(2:45:13 - 2:47:41)
Chef's Death

Chef, meanwhile, remains on the boat, hiding from the rain beneath a jacket and wondering to himself whether or not it's been eight hours. He tells himself that he is asleep and dreaming that he is on this "shitty boat," and then reaches for the radio to call in the airstrike. (Although it will take several days for the planes to arrive).

In the next shot, it is nighttime and raining heavily and the viewer sees the footsteps of Colonel Kurtz approaching Willard's place of imprisonment. Willard is no longer on the inside of his bamboo cage but somehow tied up on the outside of it and seated in a cross-legged position. He looks miserable.

Kurtz approaches him, having applied the same Tiger-stripe face camouflage which we had seen Lance wearing earlier in the film. He looks down at Willard, seeming to contemplate him for a moment, then raises his head, as though having made a decision. In the flickering yellow firelight Kurtz walks around Willard's cage from behind and then, as though to make sure he doesn't see it coming, drops Chef's severed head into his lap and walks away.

Willard screams when he recognizes Chef and uses his legs to bounce the head out of his lap into the mud in front of him.

The scene is short, but it is an important one, for it is necessary for Kurtz to demonstrate to Willard a concrete instance of his insanity. The viewer, thus far, has seen the results of many of Kurtz's murderous decisions, since the compound is strewn with the corpses of those who have been misfortunate enough to cross Kurtz's path. But now the viewer is shown an instance of Kurtz's sadism and lunacy in action.

Kurtz, in placing the head of Willard's companion in his lap, wants Willard to know *precisely* what Kurtz is capable of. He wishes to show Willard just how excessive his excesses can be, so that Willard can have all the data in front of him before he makes up his mind, out of his own free will, to put Kurtz to death in order to end the acts of insanity that radiate from him like rays from the sun.

Kurtz, in making himself up in tiger-stripe camouflage, furthermore, has devolved to the becoming-animal of the Tiger, as we have already said earlier in comment on the significance of the Tiger scene. Chef has, throughout the narrative, demonstrated his cowardice repeatedly, and is therefore not fit to be a member of Kurtz's regiment. He is an alien element that must be disposed of, and so Kurtz transforms into the very Tiger that originally threatened Chef in the film's first half and, as it were, bites off his head.

Chef's animal, as also remarked, is the snake and in mythology the gods who are associated with serpents are the dying and reviving gods like Orpheus (whose beloved Eurydice is bitten by a snake; Orpheus later loses his head and becomes an oracle), for the snake is the lunar animal that sheds its skin. As an animal that crawls along the ground, furthermore, it has an earthly valency in opposition to the bird or the dragon. (The Tiger, too, has an earthly valency).

Chef's death, furthermore, is a kind of death by air (or lack of it), just as Clean had been buried in the earth and the Chief in water.

So in this scene, we are provided with concrete proof that the instances of madness which the crew has encountered all throughout the narrative have indeed been radiating from the sa-

distic mind of Colonel Kurtz, who has become a kind of dreaming god from whom madness radiates across the entire landscape
of the war in the form of various depraved acts.

(2:47:42 - 2:53:11)
Willard's Release from His Imprisonment

Willard awakens in the gloom of what appears to be an empty trash dumpster. There is a jagged gash in the metal of the dumpster's walls through which children, together with Kurtz, are peering in at him, and through which a shaft of sunlight enters and touches his body as though to rejuvenate it. He is no longer bound, significantly, and now Kurtz, in broad daylight, opens the twin doors of the dumpster surrounded by Asian children. For the first time, the viewer gets a clear look at him: bald, wearing a black shirt and black trousers, dogtags around his neck and apparently sane. He sits down and reads to Willard an article from *Time* magazine that is dated September 22nd, 1967 and which discusses the optimism of Lyndon Johnson regarding the build- up of American troops in Vietnam only two and a half years into the war (note that this is before the Tet Offensive in January of 1968, when the tide of public opinion began to turn pessimistic regarding the war).

He reads a second article, undated, about a man named Sir Robert Thompson who led successful campaigns against communists in Malaya and subsequently became a RAND corporation consultant and then returned to Vietnam under President Nixon, where he said that things now "felt much better and smelled much better" to him over there. Kurtz then asks how things smell to Willard now?

Then he tells Willard that he is now free to move about, although he will be under guard and that he is not to attempt to escape or he will be shot. He gives him the *Time* magazine articles to read and tells him not to lose them and that they will discuss these things later. Then he gets up and leaves.

Willard, now released from bondage, attempts to stand up, but he is too weak and malnourished to stand on his own and collapses at the entrance to the dumpster.

This is the only scene which was added to the entire Kurtz compound sequence in *Apocalypse Now Redux*, but it shows the resurrection of Willard from out of the Underworld torments that Kurtz has thus far put him through. Kurtz, as Hopper correctly surmised, did indeed have something special planned for Willard, and put him through an initiatory ordeal of death and resurrection. Willard's old self as an assassin functioning essentially as an extension of the US Army has now been shed like a snakeskin. *That* Willard, whose entire life depended on being given assignments to kill people by the Army is over and done with. The new Willard is reborn as an Individual who has been unplugged from the paternal authority of the military and given a new sense of self. He can now proceed to construct a new identity independently of the authority of the Name of the Father and allow the process of creating new significations to take place.

His alliance with the Mother and the codes of the jungle has put him in touch with the *Abgrund* abysses within him, from out of which a New Self, free and autonomous and capable of making the moral decision to kill or not to kill Kurtz on his own can take place.

The Hollow Men

Willard, too weak to stand on his own, is dragged inside of Kurtz's temple by the guards, and he is fed rice by a woman who may be one of Kurtz's consorts. Through a montage of scenes–wind blowing tapestries across Buddhist stone carvings; a woman sitting with legs folded under her like a statue; Willard examining Kurtz's things–Coppola creates a sense of the passing of a number of days without aim or purpose, giving to the scene a kind of Asiatic timelessness.

Kurtz is shown seated in a haze of dusty yellow sunlight reading from T.S. Eliot's poem "The Hollow Men." "We are the hollow men," he intones, "We are the stuffed men / Leaning together / Headpiece filled with straw." But Hopper, meanwhile, discourses in typical rambling fashion to Willard about "dialectics," and his discourse is so loud that it irritates Kurtz into throwing an object at him and calling him a "mut." Hopper is intimidated and says, "This is the way the fuckin' world ends! Look at this shit we're in! Not with a bang but with a whimper and with a whimper, I'm splittin,' Jack!" Then he gets up and leaves Willard alone to listen to Kurtz's recitation.

More montage follows, and on the voice-over narration Willard tells us that while on the river he thought he'd know what to do the minute he looked at Kurtz, but it just didn't happen that way. Willard tells us that he was in there with Kurtz for days, not under guard, and free to move about. But he also says that Kurtz knew he wasn't going to go anywhere and that in fact he knew more about what Willard was going to do than Willard himself did.

Willard wonders if the generals back at Nha Trang could see Kurtz now if they'd still want him dead? More than ever, probably. Kurtz had broken from them and then he'd broken from himself. Willard says that he had never seen a man so broken up and ripped apart.

There follows a long monologue in which Kurtz tells Willard that he has seen the same horrors Willard has seen, but that Willard has no right to call him a murderer. He has the right to kill him, but not the right to judge him.

Kurtz then goes into a discourse about "horror," and says that he remembers when he was with Special Forces how he and his men went into a camp to inoculate some children. When they'd left the camp after inoculating the children for polio, an old man came running after them crying and when Kurtz and his men returned to the camp, he saw how the native soldiers had come and hacked off every inoculated arm and threw them into a little pile. Kurtz says the episode traumatized him until he realized, as though he were shot with a diamond bullet through his forehead, the *genius* of the act. My *God*, he says, the will they had to do that! These were moral men who had families and fought with their hearts, but they had the strength to do what needed to be done. Kurtz then assures Willard—and this is consistent with his dossier on "Commitment and Counter-Insurgency"—that if Kurtz had ten divisions of men like that, then the war would be won very quickly.

He then tells Willard that if he were to be killed, he would want someone to go find his son and try to explain what Kurtz had tried to be. He should tell Kurtz's son everything that Kurtz did and everything that Willard saw him do because there's nothing that he detests more than the stench of lies.

The irony, then, is that though Kurtz has put Willard through an initiatory ordeal in which he has taught him how to think for himself and to arrive at the decision to kill him out of his own free will and not as an agent of the military–from whose paternal authority Willard has by now come completely unplugged–Kurtz himself has become a "hollow man." That is to say, he is a man who has used up all his options and exhausted all his potentialities until no decision that he executes makes sense any longer. Every act, every thought, every word, is soaked in madness and he is incapable of making decisions that make sense. He has become a sadist hiding behind the guise of morality, but at the true core of his being, his *Abgrund*–at the very heart of the abyss of darkness within him–there is only what Heidegger termed "the Nothing."[43] He is a man without a soul and without a core who has used himself up. He may not have begun that way, but he has most certainly ended that way and Kurtz knows that he is mentally ill and should be put out of his misery.

If, furthermore, Kurtz is the god whose dream is the madness and lunacy of the Vietnam war which Willard has just had a guided tour through, then by killing him, perhaps Willard can end the insanity. There exists–on a purely metaphoric level, of course–the possibility that the Waste Land of the war has been the dream of a madman whose ideas have somehow externalized into three dimensional space and time, and therefore if he is killed, then the disease that radiates like a pulsing heart sending out emanations of darkness from his compound will be brought to an end.

But this requires an act of free will. The killing must be undertaken as part of a conscious decision on Willard's part, not as a "hollow man" simply carrying out orders from the higher ups, but as a moral man with a conscience who is capable of acting from out of the very *Abgrund*, or Mother-ground abyss at the center of *his* being, which is "hollow" no longer.

133

Hence, the two have traded positions: Kurtz, whose name in German—as Conrad points out in his novel—means "short," began as a man full of ideals, talent and genius who climbed his way up through the military hierarchy and then, beginning with Operation Archangel began to trace out a line of flight that led him into acts of autonomy and free will on his own part. But those very acts also led him into the center of the jungle which then began to corrupt and overcode him with *its* ancient darknesses, and Kurtz gradually, over time, became a lunatic, a hollow man without any kind of moral position to stand behind whatsoever. The Nothing—which Heidegger tells us is the very opposite of "Being"—grew from the center of his being like a seed and began, over time, to possess him and render every action corrupt with "primordiality," or the Adamic codes that still lie dormant at the heart of the jungle's ancient darknesses, a core with codes that are completely alien to those of the civilized order.

Willard, on the other hand, as we saw in the opening scene, began as a kind of "hollow man" living a life without purpose, acting only as an extension of the will of the US Army and killing the people which it told him to kill unquestioningly and simply living to thrive on the adrenalin of completing those missions, whether they were morally correct actions or not.

But with Kurtz's help, Willard has come unplugged from the Lacanian paternal order, the Big Other of the military, and managed to find within the *Abgrund* abyss of his own being a core of freewill that will allow him to execute the deed, not on behalf of the military, but for his *own* moral reasons. Willard knows, and clearly understands, that Kurtz has become a hollow man at the core, a man who has lost all purpose, aim and direction in his life and can only radiate toxicity outward into the world. Kurtz knows this, too, and he is ready to acquiesce as a willing sacrifice, but only to a man whose actions are his own.

Willard has found the "heart of darkness" within himself as the Schellingian "abyss of freedom" from out of which he can now act, as he begins to prepare to sacrifice Colonel Kurtz in ritual fashion.[44]

The Sacrifice

Willard is lying in the boat with a large hunting knife in his
hand while a voice comes over the radio: "PBR Streetgang, this
is Almighty, do you copy, over?" It is the military awaiting final
confirmation for the airstrike, but Willard turns off the radio and
his voiceover narration tells us that they were going to make him
a Major for the killing of Kurtz, but he wasn't even "in their fuckin' Army anymore." He tells us that Kurtz was waiting for him
and that even the jungle wanted him dead. He just wanted to go
out like a soldier and not like some poor wasted rag-assed ren-
egade. (Which is, however, precisely how Conrad's Kurtz dies: as
Marlow is transporting him via steamboat back to civilization, he
is already sick with an illness and dies en route).

Willard dives over the boat into the river water, and when
he surfaces again from the river, a flash of lightning illuminates
his tiger-stripe camouflaged face, the same camouflage Kurtz had
worn when he had killed Chef. (The tiger in Asian myth is always
a patron of soldiers). The song by the Doors, "The End," resumes
playing on the soundtrack as Willard sneaks up to Kurtz's temple
in the middle of a massive tribal festival, whose central act will be
the sacrifice of a water buffalo.

Another flash of lightning reveals Willard standing in black
silhouette on the steps of Kurtz's temple. He has traded his hunting knife out for a huge machete (thereby recovering the long-
lost Lacanian Phallus and *reversing* the castration which was so
important to Lacan for the individual to be able to "signify" in

a functioning society. In reality, though, Lacan's castration is a form of submission to the paternal authority of the Big Other which society represents, for a successful castration, according to him, must result in giving up desire for the Mother and acceding to the Name of the Father. All that is being dismantled, undone and reversed in Coppola's climactic sequence, which retrieves the Imaginary order of myth and symbol and draws an X over Lacan's symbolic order of linguistic signifiers designed specifically to neutralize images. Lacan's famous L-schema comes apart under the impact of the Great Myth of the Tauroctony which Coppola uses to structure his finale).

Coppola's montage goes back and forth between the Montagnards dancing and playing music while waving their spears as they approach the bull, while Willard slits the throat of Kurtz's guard, and then slowly enters into Kurtz's yellow-orange candle-lit quarters where he is in the midst of making a recording: "They train young men to drop bombs," he says into a microphone, "But their commanders won't allow them to write the word 'fuck' on their airplanes because it's obscene..."

Kurtz trails off in mid-sentence when he realizes that Willard has come for him at last, not with a gun—since that would perpetuate and fulfill his military contract—but with the same type of machete used in the ritual killing of the bull. The jungle's semiotics have recoded Willard's mission as an assassination into a ritual sacrifice with willing participation on both the parts of Kurtz and Willard.

As the tribesmen begin to slice their machetes into the bull, Willard hacks into Kurtz simultaneously, cutting him to pieces. "The End" plays appropriately over the soundtrack while the double sacrifice takes place. Once Kurtz is down and bleeding to death, he is able to mutter the final words, "the horror, the horror," which were also the last words of Conrad's Kurtz. They are fitting words since all Kurtz could see—as his final monologue

138

had demonstrated–was the horror of life, its Dionysiac abysses of death and suffering. No Nietzschean Apollonian compensation of art was available to him to balance the one-sided gaze, for art, according to Nietzsche in *The Birth of Tragedy*, is life's great compensation for its abyssal horrors. For the great philosopher of nihilism, the antidote to horror was Beauty.[45]

But for the great German philosophers who had preceded Nietzsche, the antidote to the mechanistic laws of the universe uncovered by science was, beginning with Kant's *Critique of Pure Reason*, the freedom of the will, which the philosophers Kant, Hegel and Schelling argued as the core of Being. This was especially Schelling's great insight, that each human being contains an "abyss of freedom" within him, and it is this which Willard has discovered as the antidote to the horrors he has seen. (Hence the name "Willard" with its first half, emphasizing the free act of "will" that he arrives at to kill Kurtz, not under the authority of the Name of the Father but out of the *Abgrund* of the Mother within).

While going through Kurtz's things, Willard presently finds a manuscript and flips through the pages. On one of them, scrawled in red ink, Kurtz has written: "Drop the bomb! Exterminate them all!" The latter phrase is also taken from Conrad's novel.

Willard picks up the manuscript and approaches the temple entrance, where he notices that all the tribesmen have gathered and are now awaiting him expectantly as the New Kurtz. Instead of assuming his place as Kurtz's successor, however, he tosses aside the machete and walks down the steps. The tribesmen, in imitation of his action, start throwing down their weapons and as Willard makes his way through the crowd, he spots Lance, takes his hand and they go back to the boat.

On the boat, the Army is still attempting to contact them to confirm the airstrike: "PBR Streetgang, this is Almighty, do you copy, over?"

Willard turns off the radio as he backs the boat out and heads downriver. He is no longer an extension of the US Army and its machinations. The assemblage of Willard plus military megamachine has now been severed by the very machete which Kurtz used in place of an army-issued pistol, to kill Kurtz.

During the end credits of the original theatrical release in 1979, the airstrike was shown coming in, blowing up Kurtz's compound, but in the 2001 version, the film ends only with the sound of rain hissing on the soundtrack. Then the credits come up on a dark background, minus the images of the explosions.

So, the assassination that had been given to Willard as an assignment has now been recoded by the semiotics of the jungle into a ritual sacrifice. It is, furthermore, as we have remarked, an act of free will, arrived at by Willard on his own because, as he says, he was no longer *in* their Army anymore. The paternal authority of the symbolic order has been undermined by the alliance with the Mother and her realm of the abyss. When Willard picks up the machete, he retrieves the castrated Lacanian phallus, and in using it to perform a modern equivalent of an ancient myth, recodes Lacan with Jungian semiotics.

The bull sacrifice is indeed, incredibly ancient. In the Zoroastrian creation myth, for instance, after the creator god, Ahura Mazda, creates the cosmic bull and the first man, Gayomart, the great antagonist Angra Mainyu kills the bull and then slays the cosmic man. From out of the slain bull's spinal marrow grows up all the world's food plants, while from out of its spilled semen come all the animals. Meanwhile, the decaying body of Gayomart gives rise to all the world's metals. The formula is a simple one: from death comes new life.[46]

Willard approaches Kurtz-as-bull, though, wearing the tiger stripe camouflage which Kurtz had worn when he'd beheaded Chef. The image of the solar lion slaying the lunar bull is also ubiquitous, originating in Mesopotamia before the lion became extinct there (it was hunted by kings to extinction), but the tiger functions as a semiotic equivalent, although it is a chthonic, rather than a solar symbol. Killing Kurtz, however, releases the dragon from the underworld which now rises up to deliver the life-fertilizing rains that will heal the Waste Land of the war.

The natives, in accordance with the Myth, expect Willard to take over Kurtz's role as king of his domain. But Willard's act was a *free* act, arrived at by conscious deliberation and careful thinking. It was not an act bound to the wheel of myth, which simply revolves in circles, endlessly, but rather a singularity, and as such, Willard has no desire to perpetuate Kurtz's role as the Lord of the Underworld and king of the atrocities of the Vietnam War. His act of tossing down the recovered phallus (machete) is an action that cuts the mythical circularity of the repetition of events, and in walking away from the temple and its crowd of devotees, he leaves the mythical consciousness structure behind and moves into the realm of freedom of the will and acts of singularity. It is the Philosophy of the Event–which begins with the later Heidegger and then transmigrates into French po-mo thought–as opposed to the Philosophy of Eternal Return.

When he gets back to the boat, Willard turns off the radio connecting the PBR to the Army megamachine because, as he has told us, he isn't *in* the Army anymore. He has been transformed through an initiatory ordeal into a true individual capable of generating creative acts of freedom from out of the abysses within himself and a puppet, or "hollow man," no longer.

His life is now, perhaps for the first time, his own.

Endnotes

Preface for Those with an Aversion to "Theory"

1 See John David Ebert, *Post-Classic Cinema* (Create Space, 2013).

Introduction by Way of an Answer to the Question, "How Do *You* Know what the Artist Meant?"

2 See "L-schema" in Dylan Evans, *An Introductory Dictionary of Lacanian Psychoanalysis* (London & New York: Routledge, 1996), 172.

3 Miller, Jacques-Alain, ed., Jacques Lacan, *The Psychoses: The Seminar of Jacques Lacan, Book III 1955-1956* (London & New York: Routledge, 1993), 215.

4 Gilles Deleuze and Felix Guattari, *Anti-Oedipus: Capitalism and Schizophrenia* (New York: Penguin Books, 2009).

5 Gilles Deleuze, *Masochism: Coldness and Cruelty* (New York: Zone Books, 1991), 57ff.

6 John David Ebert, *Celluloid Heroes & Mechanical Dragons: Film as the Mythology of Electronic Society* (Christchurch, New Zealand: Cybereditions, 2005), 21ff.

7 Martin Heidegger, *Basic Writings* (New York: Harper Perennial, 2008), 111ff.

8 See Timothy Morton, *Hyperobjects: Philosophy and Ecology After the End of the World* (MN: University of Minnesota Press, 2013).

9 Hans-Georg Gadamer, *Truth and Method* (London & New York: Continuum, 2006).

10 Ibid., 135.

11 See "Signature, Event, Context," in Jacques Derrida, *Margins of Philosophy* (Great Britain: Harvester Press Limited, 1982), 307ff.

12 See the essay, "The End of Philosophy?" in Cornelius Castoriadis, *Philosophy, Politics, Autonomy* (London and New York: Oxford University Press, 1991), 13ff.

13 Cornelius Castoriadis, *The Imaginary Institution of Society*, (UK: Polity Press, 2005), 135ff.

14 See "Imaginary and Imagination at the Cross-Roads," in Cornelius Castoriadis, *Figures of the Thinkable*, (online version), 123ff.

On Willard's Self-Destruction

15 Michael Herr, *Dispatches* (New York: Vintage International, 1991).

16 See the important essay summing up Castoriadis's ideas, "Imaginary and Imagination at the Cross-Roads" in Cornelius Castoriadis, *Figures of the Thinkable*, especially 145-46.

17 Michael Aaron Kamins, *Absences: Poetry* (Create Space, 2014), 3.

18 See also the short essay which Deleuze wrote summing up the main ideas of his book, "From Sacher-Masoch to Masochism," *Angelaki: Journal of the Theoretical Humanities*, vol. 9, number 1, April, 2004, 127-128.

19 See the essay "What Are Poets For?" in Martin Heidegger, *Poetry, Language, Thought* (New York: Harper Perennial, 2001), 87ff.

20 See "The Cursing of Agade" in the Electronic Text Corpus of Sumerian Literature, which can be found online at: http://etcsl.orinst.ox.ac.uk/section2/tr215.htm

The Mission

21 See the interesting YouTube video, "Superpower for Hire: Rise of the Private Military," at: https://www.youtube.com/watch?v=6LaSD8oFBZE

22 Jean Gebser, *The Ever-Present Origin* (Ohio University Press, 1985).

Bird / Snake

23 James Hillman, *Revisioning Psychology* (New York: Harper Perennial, 1992), 115ff.

24 Albert B. Lord, *The Singer of Tales* (Harvard University Press, 2000).

25 Caroline Alexander, *The War That Killed Achilles* (New York: Viking Penguin, 2009).

26 Walter Ong, *Orality and Literacy* (New York: Routledge, 2012), 147.

Kilgore I

27 See "WikiLeaks and the Death of Culture" in John David Ebert, *The New Media Invasion: Digital Technologies and the World They Unmake* (Jefferson, North Carolina: McFarland and Co., 2011), 78ff.

28 Ibid., "Robots, Drones and the Disappearance of the Human Being," 156ff.

29 For the gigantification effects of electric media on the celebrity, see John David Ebert, *Dead Celebrities, Living Icons: Tragedy and Fame in the Age of the Multimedia Superstar* (New York: Praeger / Greenwood, 2010).

Kilgore II

30 See my earlier reading of this sequence, "Apocalypse Now as a Celluloid Book of the Dead," in John David Ebert, *Celluloid Heroes, Mechanical Dragons*, ibid., 21ff.

31 See "1227: Treatise on Nomadology–The War Machine," in Gilles Deleuze and Felix Guattari, *A Thousand Plateaus: Capitalism and Schizophrenia* (University of Minnesota Press, 1987), 351ff.

Mango / Tiger Interlude

32 Lewis Mumford, *The City in History: Its Origins, Its Transformations and its Prospects* (New York: Harcourt, 1961), 3ff.

Playboy Bunnies

33 For the concept of Maximal Stress, see Heiner Muhlmann, *MSC: Maximal Stress Cooperation, the Driving Force of Cultures* (New York: Springer-Verlag, 2005).

Third Dossier

34 For the concepts of "rhizome" vs. "arborescent" see "Introduction: Rhizome" in Deleuze & Guattari, *A Thousand Plateaus*, ibid., 3ff.

35 For the concept of "becoming-animal," see "1732: Becoming-Intense, Becoming-Animal, Becoming-Imperceptible..." in Deleuze & Guattari, *A Thousand Plateaus*, ibid., 232ff.

Medevac

36 There is a deleted scene from the film known as "Monkey Sampan," which was never put back into the film, but it is

a deliberate homage to Herzog's *Aguirre,* since it shows a sampan overrun with monkeys floating past the PBR, just as the final image of *Aguirre* shows the mad leader alone on his raft, his entire crew dead, with an army of monkeys swarming across the raft.

37 Gadamer, ibid., 365-66.

38 See the essay "Differance" in Jacques Derrida, *Margins of Philosophy,* ibid., 1ff.

The Do Lung Bridge

39 See the essay "Letter on Humanism" for Heidegger's concept of the "unhoming" of Modern Man in Martin Heidegger, *Basic Writings,* ibid., 213ff.

40 For the concepts of the "grafting" and "folding" of texts within texts, see the essay "Dissemination," in Jacques Derrida, *Dissemination* (UK: the Athlone Press, 1981), 287ff.

The Chief's Death

41 For this concept of the "primitive territorial sign regime," see "The Primitive Territorial Machine," in Deleuze and Guattari, *Anti-Oedipus,* ibid, 145ff.

Willard's Imprisonment

42 The best example of this myth is "The Hymn of the Pearl," and an excellent explication of it is given in Hans Jonas, *The Gnostic Religion* (Boston: Beacon Press, 2001), 112ff.

The Hollow Men

43 For Heidegger's concept of "the Nothing," see the essay "What is Metaphysics?" in Martin Heidegger, *Basic Writings*, ibid., 89ff.

44 For Schelling's theory of the "abyss of freedom," the reader should consult F.W.J. Schelling, *Philosophical Investigations Into the Essence of Human Freedom* (New York: SUNY Press, 2006).

The Sacrifice

45 For the concept of art as the compensation for the Dionsiac abyss, see Friedrich Nietzsche, "The Birth of Tragedy," in Walter Kaufmann, ed., *The Basic Writings of Nietzsche* (New York: Modern Library, 1968), 42-44.

46 For the basic Zoroastrian myth, see Mircea Eliade, *A History of Religious Ideas Volume 2: From Gautama Buddha to the Triumph of Christianity*, (University of Chicago Press, 1982), 317-18.

Bibliography

Alexander, Caroline. *The War That Killed Achilles*. New York: Viking, 2009.

Castoriadis, Cornelius. *The Imaginary Institution of Society*. UK: Polity Press, 2005.

____, *Figures of the Thinkable*. Stanford University Press, 2007.

____, *Philosophy, Politics, Autonomy*. London and New York: Oxford University Press, 1991.

Deleuze, Gilles. *Masochism: Coldness and Cruelty*. New York: Zone Books, 1991.

____, "From Sacher-Masoch to Masochism." *Angelaki: Journal of the Theoretical Humanities*, Vol. 9, No. 1, April, 2004.

____, and Guattari, Felix. *Anti-Oedipus: Capitalism and Schizophrenia*. New York: Penguin Books, 2009.

____, and ____. *A Thousand Plateaus: Capitalism and Schizophrenia*. University of Minnesota Press, 1987.

Derrida, Jacques. *Dissemination*. UK: the Athlone Press, 1981.

____. *Margins of Philosophy*. UK: Harvester Press Limited, 1982.

Ebert, John David. *Celluloid Heroes & Mechanical Dragons: Film as the Mythology of Electronic Society*. Christchurch, New Zealand: Cybereditions, 2005.

____, *Dead Celebrities, Living Icons: Tragedy and Fame in the Age of the Multimedia Superstar*. New York: Praeger / Greenwood, 2010.

_____, *The New Media Invasion: Digital Technologies and the World They Unmake*. Jefferson, North Carolina: McFarland and Co., 2011.

_____, *Post-Classic Cinema*. Create Space. 2011.

Eliade, Mircea. *A History of Religious Ideas Volume 2: From Gautama Buddha to the Triumph of Christianity*. University of Chicago Press, 1982.

Evans, Dylan. *An Introductory Dictionary of Lacanian Psychoanalysis*. London & New York: Routledge, 1996.

Gadamer, Hans-Georg. *Truth and Method*. London & New York: Continuum, 2006.

Gebser, Jean. *The Ever-Present Origin*. Ohio Universisty Press, 1985.

Heidegger, Martin. *Basic Writings*. New York: Harper Perennial, 2008.

_____, *Poetry, Language, Thought*. New York: Harper Perennial, 2001.

Herr, Michael. *Dispatches*. New York: Vintage International, 1991.

Hillman, James. *Revisioning Psychology*. New York: Harper Perennial, 1992.

Jonas, Hans. *The Gnostic Religion*. Boston: Beacon Press, 2001.

Kamins, Michael Aaron. *Absences: Poetry*. Create Space, 2014.

Lord, Albert B. *The Singer of Tales*. Harvard University Press, 2000.

Miller, Jacques-Alain, ed., *Jacques Lacan, The Psychoses: The Seminar of Jacques Lacan, Book III 1955-1956*. London & New York: Routledge, 1993.

Morton, Timothy. *Hyperobjects: Philosophy and Ecology After the End of the World*. MN: University of Minnesota Press, 2013.

Muhlmann, Heiner. MSC: Maximal Stress Cooperation, the Driving Force of Cultures. New York: Springer-Verlag, 2005.

Nietzsche, Friedrich. *The Basic Writings of Nietzsche*. New York: Modern Library, 1968.

Mumford, Lewis. *The City in History: Its Origins, Its Transformations and its Prospects*. New York: Harcourt, 1961.

Ong, Walter. *Orality and Literacy*. New York: Routledge, 2012.

Schelling, F.W.J. *Philosophical Investigations Into the Essence of Human Freedom*. New York: SUNY Press, 2006.

CPSIA information can be obtained at www.ICGtesting.com
Printed in the USA
LVOW10s1524251015

459665LV00001B/113/P

9 780985 480288